Authors' Acknowledgements

From Kate: The seeds for this book were sown long ago, so I'd like to acknowledge my teachers who got me curious about this elusive concept of confidence and Margaret who asked the powerful question I wanted to answer: 'So where do you keep your confidence?'

Writing another book is like having another baby. It seems like a great idea until you are giving birth and then a joy when it's safely delivered. My special thanks go to my writing partner Brinley who adopted this concept with me. To all my family and friends I appreciate your continual love and support. Bob – you're a star.

To my clients, colleagues and coaches, thank you for the stories, inspiration and support. To Dan, Kathleen, Sam, and Jason plus all at Wiley, thank you for your cool, calm confidence over the hurdles.

Now it's over to you the reader to make this book really work for you. Please take the baby now and run with it!

From Brinley: After a long and relatively conventional business career it is an amazing thing to reconnect with the passions and drivers of my youth and find them all as fresh as they were in the 1970s and bursting for their opportunity to be fully expressed in the world. This has been my experience over the last 4–5 years and I am grateful to everyone who has played a part in my awakening.

My mission now is to be an awakener to anyone who feels there should be the opportunity for a full and rich life that integrates home and work and which doesn't 'cost the earth'.

My special thanks go to Kate for this opportunity to work with her, the Wiley publishing team, and to my wife Nicola, mother of our two young children. I also want to acknowledge my older children Loretta and Oliver for their wonderful inspiration and love over the last 20 years, and my parents who raised me to think for myself.

I encourage you, the reader, to take on your work in the world with a renewed confidence and sense of purpose. The world is changing and it needs to change further and faster. With your commitment we can make it happen.

Publisher's Acknowledgements

We're proud of this book; please send us your comments at http://dummies.custhelp.com. For other comments, please contact our Customer Care Department within the U.S. at 877-762-2974, outside the U.S. at 317-572-3993, or fax 317-572-4002.

Some of the people who helped bring this book to market include the following:

Acquisitions, Editorial, and Vertical Websites

Project Editor: Steven Edwards

(Previous Edition: Daniel Mersey)

Commissioning Editor: Kerry Laundon

Assistant Editor: Ben Kemble

Development Editor: Charlie Wilson

Proofreader: Kim Vernon

Production Manager: Daniel Mersey

Publisher: David Palmer

Cover Photos: © iStock / Sean Nel

Cartoons: Rich Tennant
(www.the5thwave.com)

Composition Services

Project Coordinator: Kristie Rees

Layout and Graphics: Melanee Habig

Proofreaders: Lauren Mandelbaum, Dwight Ramsey

Indexer: Sharon Shock

Publishing and Editorial for Consumer Dummies

    Kathleen Nebenhaus, Vice President and Executive Publisher

    Kristin Ferguson-Wagstaffe, Product Development Director

    Ensley Eikenburg, Associate Publisher, Travel

    Kelly Regan, Editorial Director, Travel

Publishing for Technology Dummies

    Andy Cummings, Vice President and Publisher

Composition Services

    Debbie Stailey, Director of Composition Services

Confidence

FOR

DUMMIES®

2ND EDITION

by Kate Burton and Brinley Platts

A John Wiley and Sons, Ltd, Publication

Confidence For Dummies®, 2nd Edition

Published by
John Wiley & Sons, Ltd
The Atrium
Southern Gate
Chichester
West Sussex
PO19 8SQ
England
www.wiley.com

For general information on our other products and services, please contact our Customer Care Department within the U.S. at 877-762-2974, outside the U.S. at 317-572-3993, or fax 317-572-4002.

For technical support, please visit www.wiley.com/techsupport.

Wiley publishes in a variety of print and electronic formats and by print-on-demand. Some material included with standard print versions of this book may not be included in e-books or in print-on-demand. If this book refers to media such as a CD or DVD that is not included in the version you purchased, you may download this material at http://booksupport.wiley.com. For more information about Wiley products, visit www.wiley.com.

British Library Cataloguing in Publication Data: A catalogue record for this book is available from the British Library

ISBN 978-1-118-31467-8 (pbk); ISBN 978-1-118-31468-5 (ebk); ISBN 978-1-118-31469-2 (ebk); ISBN 978-1-118-31470-8 (ebk)

Printed and bound in Great Britain by TJ International, Padstow, Cornwall

10 9 8 7 6 5 4 3 2 1

About the Authors

Kate Burton (see www.kateburton.co.uk) is an international Neuro-linguistc Programming master coach who challenges individuals and organisations to create lives that are sustainable and fun. Her business career began in corporate advertising and marketing with Hewlett-Packard. Now, she works with leaders and managers across industries and cultures to enable them to work at their best. Kate loves to deliver custom-built coaching programmes that support people to boost their communication skills, motivation, self-awareness, and confidence. She believes that people all have unique talents, abilities, and core values; the skill is about honouring them to the full.

In addition to co-authoring *Neuro-linguistic Programming For Dummies, Neuro-linguistic Programming Workbook For Dummies,* and *Confidence For Dummies,* Kate is the author of *Live Life, Love Work* (published by Capstone, a John Wiley & Sons imprint). Her latest addition to the *For Dummies* personal development range is *Coaching with NLP For Dummies.*

Brinley N. Platts is a leading executive coach, researcher, and consultant to FTSE 100 companies. He is one of the UK's leading authorities on CIO and IT executive careers and works with international companies on the integration of senior executive life and career goals. He is a behavioural scientist by training, and his passion is to enable large organisations to become places where ordinary decent people can grow and express their talents freely to the benefit of all stakeholders. He is a co-founder of the Bring YourSELF to Work campaign, which aims to release the pent-up talent and passion of today's global workforce to create the better world we all desire and want our children to inherit.

Contents at a Glance

Contents

Introduction

● ●

Confidence is one of those odd things in life that turn out to be surprisingly difficult to tie down (beauty and quality belong to this strange, subjective group too). You may think that you know what it is, and you may feel certain that you can recognise it when you see it, but you may struggle to define exactly what 'it' is.

Confidence is an everyday experience, something you have quite often, except on those all-important occasions when it seems to leave you and you could really use more of it – whatever 'it' is. Whether you're a mature business person or a school leaver, confidence has this annoying habit of disappearing unexpectedly. Yet when you really need to dig deep, you find you have amazing internal strength to draw on from your toughest life experiences. In this newly updated second edition of *Confidence For Dummies*, you can clear up the confusion around confidence, and particularly what you may refer to as self-confidence. You dispel a lot of the mystique around how you can develop and build your self-confidence; perhaps to an extent you feared would never be possible for you.

We've designed every chapter of this book to help you understand: where your personal confidence comes from, how you can generate an incredibly powerful type of confidence in your life on demand, and how you can do it more reliably with less stress. You will make the fastest progress by immediately putting what you discover into action, by trying out the advice and exercises as you go along, and thereby achieving the deep and lasting personal confidence you were born to enjoy.

Are you up for this? Let's go.

About This Book

Type the word 'confidence' into an Internet search engine and you can expect over 50 million hits. That's a lot of published material about something so natural. Those hits are also an indication of the breadth of the subject so, as you want to get straight to the heart of your confidence, we have been selective in *Confidence For Dummies.*

The task ahead of you is to build your confidence so that you can be more powerful, more engaging, and more at ease in every aspect of your life. These areas include your work and your private life (friends and family, romance, community, and so on). We steer clear of more complex explorations of personal development, except where they translate into immediate practical guidance.

You should be able to dip into this book for practical and rapid support on such everyday confidence problems as:

- Preparing for an important presentation or job interview.
- Asking the man or woman of your dreams to marry you.
- Picking up the phone to make that difficult call to an important new customer.
- Asking for the order, if you're in sales.
- Picking yourself up quickly and appropriately after any setback.
- Connecting online with the wider world through tweets and blogs.

Conventions Used in This Book

To help you navigate through this book, we set up a few conventions:

- *Italics* are used for emphasis and to highlight new words or defined terms.
- **Bold faced** text indicates the key concept in a list.
- `Monofont` is used for web and email addresses.

What You're Not to Read

Confidence For Dummies is primarily an action guide to building your confidence. In many places, this requires us to set the context you need to grasp the situation. In other places, we include material useful for your full understanding, but not essential for you to be able to take the action and get the benefit. Much as we want you to take all of it on board in time, we make it easy for you to identify those parts that you can leave for later.

When you're short of time, or when you just want to stick with the essentials, you can skip over these sections:

- ✔ **The text in the sidebars:** The shaded boxes that appear here and there share personal stories and anecdotes, but they're not integral to your taking action, and you can safely skip reading them if you're not interested.

- ✔ **The stuff on the copyright page:** You'll find nothing here of value unless you're looking for legal notices and reprint information. If you are, then this is the place to look.

Foolish Assumptions

We make a few other assumptions about you. We assume that you're a normal human being who wants to be happy and confident. You're probably interested in becoming more effective in various parts of your life and in becoming more comfortable when you face demanding situations and people. Although you're probably already acting confidently in many areas, you may lack the power and skills to perform the way you want to in some others.

This book is for you if you want to:

- ✔ Grow in the areas where you currently feel stuck.
- ✔ Become better at your job and get acknowledged for it.
- ✔ Feel less anxious and stressed about things you have to do.
- ✔ Step up to become a powerful leader in your work or community.
- ✔ Feel confident that no matter what life throws at you, you can find a way to deal with it.

How This Book Is Organised

The book is divided into five main sections, with each of these sections broken into chapters. The table of contents gives you details on each chapter.

Part 1: Considering the Basics

In this part, we explain exactly what we mean by confidence and how it feels. You can evaluate how much confidence you have currently. You discover how to spot where your confidence is waxing or waning, in what areas of your life you need more confidence right now, and what is keeping you stuck.

Armed with all this insight, you can create your personal programme for the new super-confident version of you that you want to present to the world.

Part II: Gathering the Elements

Everyone would like to be more confident on occasion, but to take action, whether at work or socially, when you're feeling anything but confident, requires motivation. In this part, you're invited to connect with your main drivers in life, gain a better understanding of your deepest values, and leverage this information to get what you want.

You venture into the sometimes messy world of emotions and mood swings – including the extremes of ecstasy, anger, and despair. This part guides you to safe connection with your personal motivation.

Part III: Building Your Confident Self

In this part, you pull up your most confident self and reconnect with how you do it. You let go of perfectionism in pursuit of effectiveness, let go of unreal expectations to enjoy your experiences. You find out how to extend your comfort zone and become relaxed and focused in achieving whatever you want. You forge a link between your mind and body and realise that taking better care of yourself helps you maintain your self-confidence. You also discover how to project your confident self out into the world through your powerful voice. Best of all, you discover the Guaranteed Success Formula as a fool-proof approach for getting the results you really want.

Part IV: Engaging Other People

In this part of your journey to confidence, you get tips on putting your increased personal power to use at work and in your private life. You use what you know about building confidence to ensure that your approach to romantic relationships is successful, and you find out how to take the plunge into social media to form a powerful, confident online presence.

Part V: The Part of Tens

When you want a quick fix of inspiration to spur you into action or a reminder of what is important every day, you can find it here. The familiar Part of Tens gives you straight-talking confidence-boosting advice in bite-sized chunks.

Icons Used in This Book

Within each chapter you find the following icons pointing you to particular types of information that you may find immediately useful. Here is an explanation of what each icon stands for:

 This icon brings your attention to a personal story you may find inspiring or useful.

 The bull's-eye highlights practical advice you can use to boost your confidence immediately.

 This icon indicates an exercise you can use to broaden your understanding of yourself and your own confidence issues.

 Information to take note of and keep in mind as you apply your boosted confidence in the world is indicated with the finger and string.

Text next to the Warning icon urges you to take special care of yourself in dealing with specific issues.

This icon does what it says and gives you a clear definition of terms that may not be familiar to you.

Where to Go from Here

Although all the material in this book is relevant to developing your most confident version of yourself, you don't have to read it cover to cover over any set period. You benefit most if you address first those sections that are most relevant to the areas of your life where you feel the need for more self-confidence most keenly. For example, if you're feeling nervous about changes happening at work, or going to a party, say, go first to the chapters that deal with this; feel free to dip in where you need guidance and support right now.

After you read the book and are keen to take your levels of confidence and achievement to even higher levels, we recommend more personalised forms of development training and coaching. Take a look at the further guidance and resources we recommend at www.yourmostconfidentself.com.

Part I
Considering the Basics

The 5th Wave   By Rich Tennant

©RICHTENNANT

"I'm tired of letting everyone pull my strings."

In this part . . .

*F*rom understanding what confidence is and how it feels to tackling unhelpful assumptions you make about yourself, the chapters in this part help you lay the foundations for your new, confident self. Armed with all kinds of insights into what you want for yourself, savour these chapters to design your own journey and set the milestones along the way.

Chapter 1

Assessing Your Confidence

- -

In This Chapter

▶ Identifying the key ingredients of confidence

▶ Rating yourself on the confidence indicators

▶ Celebrating your good points

▶ Visualising the super-confident new you

▶ Getting started on changing

- -

*W*elcome to the start of your confidence-building pro-gramme. It's great to have you on board for what we promise will be a wonderful and transformational journey. With confidence comes more fun, freedom, and opportunities to do what really works for you.

In this chapter, we lay the foundations for our travels together, starting with some definitions of confidence and a practical, nuts-and-bolts assessment of where you are today.

Here you start flexing your confidence muscles – and we know from experience that you're already in a much more confident shape than you may give yourself credit for. You can also celebrate what you're already good at and imagine the new super-confident you on the horizon as your confidence-building work progresses.

Then, it's about getting tooled up ready for action. After all, what's the point of hiding your talents when there's so much important work to be done in this world?

Defining Confidence

When asked to think what confidence means, most people have a feel for it but find it quite difficult to tie down precisely. After all, confidence is not some miracle pill or wonder food you can buy in a shop.

Before you dive into this book on how to be more confident, we invite you to explore the definition of confidence. A good dictionary provides at least three definitions for *confidence,* and you need to understand each aspect as it is easy to muddle them:

- ✓ **Self-assuredness:** This definition relates to your confidence in your ability to perform to a certain standard.

- ✓ **Belief in the ability of other people:** This definition focuses on how you expect others to behave in a trustworthy or competent way.

- ✓ **Keeping certain information secret or restricted to a few people:** This definition concerns the idea of keeping a confidence.

We've found that an even better definition exists. One that's more useful to you in everyday life. One that's true no matter how tough a situation you face, or how comfortable you feel about it. Our definition:

> At its heart, *confidence* is the ability to take appropriate and effective action in any situation, however challenging it appears to you or others.

Confidence is not about feeling good inside, although it's a bonus if you do.

What it is in practice

Now, how does confidence show up in daily life? Well, have you ever started something – perhaps an exercise session or presentation at work – even though you didn't feel like doing it at that moment, only to find that when you got going, you started to feel okay about it and even glad you tackled it? This kind of shift in how you experience a situation gives you a taste of what confidence is in practice. It is your ability to reach beyond how you're feeling in the moment in order to take action that leads to the outcome you want.

Anish is an accountant turned management consultant who has travelled the world on international assignments for large corporations. Now running his own partnership, he leads complex projects and presents a calm, rational, and focused image in business meetings. When deadlines are pressing and tempers rise in project teams, he is the one who patiently exudes confidence that delivery can and will happen on time.

How does he do this under pressure? 'I experience the situation as a series of hoops that I just need to get through – like a tunnel,' he says. 'Sometimes there will just be two or three. At other times, as many as twenty in a row. I can feel as anxious inside about what needs to be done as the next person, but I experience it as a sequence to go through patiently one by one, and it gets easier as I see the light beckoning at the end.'

Approaching challenges with confidence in Anish's style brings clear benefits. For example:

✔ You believe that it is possible to tackle and achieve things that others consider difficult.

✔ You inspire others around you and stop them panicking.

✔ You break down a large project into smaller parts that you can tackle one by one.

How it feels

Don't worry about whether you feel comfortable performing a challenging activity or are fully relaxed about the action you're taking. Confident people are okay with the feeling of not knowing all the answers. Phew, what a relief. Confidence is just the feeling that it'll be okay.

The sense of feeling confident inside comes with increased practice and familiarity with what you do. You can also create it from your life experiences and bring it out when you need it. Doing so doesn't mean that you won't ever feel scared. You will, but the good news is that you can live with the fear.

Here are some ways that you can recognise confidence in yourself:

- ✔ You feel poised and balanced.
- ✔ You're breathing easily.
- ✔ You're moving towards a goal or action with a sense of purpose.
- ✔ You're being proactive rather than defensive.
- ✔ You know that you can deal with whatever life throws at you, even if you can't control it.
- ✔ You can laugh at yourself.
- ✔ You know everything will be alright in the end, however long it takes.

So, we're going to support you as you find your inner confidence to take the first step to wherever you want to go, however scary or difficult it seems just now.

Determining Where You Stand Now

Any measure of confidence is, by its nature, subjective. Other people may form an opinion about how confident you are based on your outside appearance and actions, and only you can know for sure what you feel like on the inside – what you believe to be true, and what it's like to be you.

In this section, we invite you to make your own assessment of where your confidence level is today.

Your confidence level is different according to the time and place. If you think back ten years to a younger you, you probably realise that your confidence has grown since then according to the experiences you've faced, knowing that you've lived to tell the tale. How confident you feel differs in various situations, and may well fluctuate from day to day and week to week according to what's happening at work and at home. There may be areas where you've taken a risk, or suffered a loss, for example, and your confidence has dropped.

If you've been unwell and have taken on too much work, your confidence level may dip and wobble. Yet when you're well and have a sense of completing your work, you may feel as if you can conquer the world. Think of your confidence as a pair of old-fashioned scales – your confidence is a delicate balancing mechanism and anything, even something feather light, may tip it either way unexpectedly.

Make change easy on yourself. Rome wasn't built in a day. We're not going to suggest that you go hang gliding off a mountain top today if standing on a stepladder gives you the collywobbles in your stomach. Allow yourself time and space to improve. Lots of smaller steps are often more realistic and maintainable compared to giant leaps for mankind.

Looking at indicators of confidence

We pinpoint ten core indicators of confidence that we explore in depth throughout this book. When you act with confidence, you're likely to have a good selection of these ten qualities:

- ✔ **Direction and values:** You know what you want, where you want to go, and what's really important to you.

- ✔ **Motivation:** You're motivated by and enjoy what you do. In fact, you're likely to get so engrossed in what you're doing that nothing distracts you.

- ✔ **Emotional stability:** You've a calm and focused approach to how you are yourself and how you are with other people as you tackle challenges. You notice difficult emotions such as anger and anxiety, but you work with them rather than letting them overcome you.

- ✔ **A positive mind-set:** You've the ability to stay optimistic and see the bright side even when you encounter setbacks. You hold positive regard for yourself as well as other people.

- ✔ **Self-awareness:** You know what you're good at, how capable you feel, and how you look and sound to others. You also acknowledge that you're a human being, and you don't expect to be perfect.

- ✔ **Flexibility in behaviour:** You adapt your behaviour according to circumstance. You can see the bigger picture as well as paying attention to details. You take other people's views on board in making decisions.

- ✔ **Eagerness to develop:** You enjoy stretching yourself, treating each day as a learning experience, rather than acting as if you're already an expert with nothing new to find out. You take your discoveries to new experiences.

- ✔ **Health and energy:** You're in touch with your body, respect it, and have a sense that your energy is flowing freely. You manage stressful situations without becoming ill.

- ✔ **A willingness to take risks:** You've the ability to act in the face of uncertainty – and put yourself on the line even when you don't have the answers or all the skills to get things right.

- ✔ **A sense of purpose:** You've an increasing sense of the coherence of the different parts of your life. You've chosen a theme or purpose for your life.

You can use these indicators to help figure out where you're stuck in life because you lack the confidence to move on.

Finding your place on the scale

The 20 statements in Table 1-1 relate to the indicators of confidence we laid out in the preceding section. Consider each and decide on the extent to which you agree or disagree using the five-point scale provided. Take the test as often as you like and keep a note of your developing profile.

Do the evaluation now and make a note in your diary to come back and review it in, say, six months' time and notice what you've discovered.

Completing this questionnaire provides you with a simple stock take of some of the main areas of your life affecting your confidence right now. If you answer the questions accurately, you can use specific chapters of this book to target the areas that merit your immediate attention.

There are no right or wrong answers. Simply answer as honestly as you can.

Frankl's search for meaning

Viktor E. Frankl, the founder of Logotherapy, was one of the 20th century's great therapists. He formulated his revolutionary approach to psychotherapy in four Nazi death camps, including Auschwitz, where he was captive from 1942 to 1945.

At the heart of his theory is the belief that, whatever our personal circumstance, what keeps us going most surely is the meaning we find in living. This belief helped him survive the camps against all odds when millions of others perished, and after the war it enabled him to treat many of its victims.

Frankl agreed with the philosopher Nietzsche that 'he who has a *why* to live for can bear with almost any *how*'. In the camps, Frankl saw that people who had hope of being reunited with loved ones, who had projects they felt a need to complete, or who had great faith tended to have a better chance at survival than those who had little to keep them going through the difficulties.

When one of Frankl's patients faced a collapse of confidence through the loss of meaning in his or her life, Frankl would seek to bring relief through three routes:

1. To broaden the patient's appreciation of life by making conscious the fuller value of all that person was achieving, creating, and accomplishing (and yet dismissing).

2. To recover and re-live powerful if transient experiences of feeling most alive: the view from a mountain top, the love for another, the perfect athletic performance (what Maslow may have called 'Peak Experiences' see Chapter 4).

3. To find a powerful positive meaning by the reframing of apparently meaningless situations. For example, a man surviving his wife after a long and happy union had saved her from the trauma he was having to bear of living alone.

Frankl's experience and his thinking are set out beautifully in his book: *Man's Search for Meaning*.

Table 1-1	Evaluating Your Confidence				
Statement	*Strongly Agree*	*Agree*	*Neutral*	*Disagree*	*Strongly Disagree*
I have a clear sense of what is important to me.					
I know what I want in life.					
I never beat myself up about my failings.					
I can stand back and think clearly when things get emotional.					
A lot of my work involves things I enjoy doing.					
I sometimes become totally engrossed in an activity.					
I am known for being optimistic.					
I respect myself and many of those around me.					
I have a realistic view of my strengths and weaknesses.					
I know what others consider to be my strengths.					
I consult others, where appropriate, before taking decisions.					

Statement	Strongly Agree	Agree	Neutral	Disagree	Strongly Disagree
I am comfortable with both the big picture and the important details of a situation.					
I enjoy doing new things and taking on fresh challenges.					
I relish the opportunity to find out new things and to grow.					
I take care of my body.					
I feel able to handle stress in my life.					
I have a healthy attitude to risk taking.					
I don't always have to have every 't' crossed and 'i' dotted before taking action.					
I sometimes meditate or think deeply about the connectedness of different parts of my life.					
I know what I am here to do. I have a chosen mission or purpose.					

Now, give yourself 5 points for every tick in the *strongly agree* column, 4 for every one in the *agree* column, 3 for *neutral*, 2 for *disagree*, and finally 1 for *strongly disagree*. Add up your points and check the next section for advice related to your total score. The second stage of the scoring process – in the 'Personal profile' section – encourages you to determine which areas of your life and this book are worthy of your immediate attention.

Overall rating

Find your total score in one of the following categories:

- ✔ **80–100: Congratulations!** By any standards, you're what most people consider to be a confident person. You're clear on your priorities and are in positive pursuit of the life you want.

  Take note of any areas where you scored below par and consider the advice in the 'Personal profile' section below.

- ✔ **60–80: Well done!** You're already pretty confident in most situations. Just a few areas bring you down in the test and in your life. You can find plenty of guidance for dealing with these trouble spots in this book. Look at the advice in the next section to make the most rapid progress.

- ✔ **40–60: You're in the right place!** You may be experiencing some confusion or uncertainty in your life right now, and you may wonder whether you can do anything about it. Give yourself time to work on the areas that need attention and you will be amazed by the progress you can make.

- ✔ **20–40: Full marks for honesty and courage!** Your confidence may be at low ebb right now, but it doesn't have to stay that way. You can find good advice that you can put to use on almost every page of this book. If you take our advice, and act upon it, you face the possibility of life transformation.

Personal profile

After you score your questionnaire and read the relevant advice in the preceding section, take another look at your scoring and note the areas that brought your overall score down. Look at statements you most strongly disagreed with.

If you scored high on most questions, look at the statements with which you find yourself unable to strongly agree.

You can use your individual scores to create your personal confidence profile. This profile now gives you something specific to think about. Let's say you're unclear about what is most important to you in life, or you beat yourself up over every little mistake. Perhaps you fail to consult others, or you feel alone and isolated. All these things affect how confident you feel, and how prepared you are to take action.

You can find advice and action guidance on all these issues in the chapters that follow. Use the contents pages and chapter summaries to find those areas that can give your confidence the quickest and biggest boosts.

 This exercise is a simple one, designed to give you a quick start and an immediate agenda for improvement. You can use the test to monitor your growing confidence. However, if you want a more detailed analysis, go to our website at www. yourmostconfidentself.com.

Recognising Your Strengths

Mark Twain said that each one of us has the substance within to achieve whatever our goals and dreams define. What we are missing are the wisdom and insight to use what we already have.

A key aspect of confident people is that they've high self-esteem – they hold themselves in positive self-regard. This means that they know how to love themselves and that they acknowledge what they're good at. These realisations boost their resilience and ability to take on greater challenges.

Your ability to take appropriate, effective action is affected by various things in your life that may seem to have little direct relation to the task at hand. Your values are a good example of this. Your self-confidence is likely to waver if you don't value what you excel at doing. Research shows that if you value what you're good at, you're likely to be highly confident in that area. If you value what you're not so good at, then you will not feel so confident, even though your friends may reassure you that this lack of confidence is not much of a problem at all.

Building confidence begins with going with your strengths. If you're great at music, don't beat yourself up because you're not going to play international rugby. Pat yourself on the back, practise accepting compliments for everything you do well, and enjoy the positive reinforcement from others. Respect and honour yourself, and you'll find that you get respect and honour from those around you.

For confidence to thrive and grow, you must concentrate your attention on what you're good at, rather than trying to turn yourself into something that you're not.

You also need to free yourself from unhelpful negative thoughts about your shortcomings or negative incidents in your life – more about that in Chapter 2.

Celebrating your own talents first

Everybody has different interests and skills. (Thank goodness for that!) So, your first step in developing confidence is to decide what you're really good at, and build on it. It's time to recognise your qualities and build up your talent store. Use the worksheet in Table 1-3 to list some of these talents that show up at work and in your home life. Record during what period of your life you best put those skills and talents to use.

The sample worksheet in Table 1-2 gives you some ideas for the kinds of strengths you can include in your own worksheet.

Table 1-2	Sample Strengths Worksheet	
Things I Am Good At	*When I Was At My Best*	*Actions I Can Put in Place to Encourage This Talent*
At work		
Strong, decisive manager at the power plant.	Put myself forward for next promotion board.	Volunteer to be press spokesperson.
Good, creative contributor in team meetings.	Suggested the new shift rota, which was adopted.	Follow through other suggestions with my boss.

Things I Am Good At	When I Was At My Best	Actions I Can Put in Place to Encourage This Talent
At home		
Telling jokes that people find funny.	Speech at my brother's wedding.	Get more funny material to do Comic Relief spot at the Arts Centre.
House improvements – I'm constantly repairing or upgrading something in the house.	New bathroom – installed all by myself in six weekends.	Agree on list of creative DIY projects with my wife.
Football coaching for John's school team.	Best results in ten sessions. Strong competition for places.	Get school team to enter for higher league.

Now, fill out Table 1-3 with your own strengths and talents.

Table 1-3	Strengths Worksheet	
Things I Am Good At	When I Was At My Best	Actions I Can Put in Place to Encourage This Talent
At work		
At home		

Decide which of these talents you'd like to make more of and what action you can take to sponsor and encourage each of your useful talents.

When you've created your list of actions, don't file them away and forget about them until next year. Instead, set a timescale for things that you're going to do in the shorter term – next week or month – and for those to do in the longer term. Chapter 3 offers advice on setting steps to achieve your goals.

Gathering feedback

Getting feedback from others is a powerful shortcut to building your confidence. Apart from performance reviews at work, you may not be in the habit of asking people to give you feedback on how you're doing, and you may be amazed at what you find out about yourself by doing so. People rarely recognise what they do well. 'Isn't everyone good at that?' they ask. Most people are their own worst critic, and it can be a wonderful experience to receive positive feedback from your nearest and dearest. Having that outside view from another person helps you uncover hidden talents.

Ask six people who have known you a while if they'd be prepared to give you some feedback. Choose people who represent the different groups in which you mix, including family members, friends, work colleagues, and those who know you from your interests in the community, church, or a sports club. Ask each of them these questions:

- ✔ What am I good at?
- ✔ When have you seen me operate at my best?
- ✔ What should I do more of?
- ✔ What should I do less of?
- ✔ What can you rely on me for?
- ✔ Where do you think that I can stretch myself?

After collecting feedback, look for the common trends and themes and think of ways to build them into your goals and development plans. If a number of people tell you similar things, it's likely there's some truth in the message and worth taking notice. (The odd negative comment from your nearest and dearest may be less helpful and more about their needs than yours – test it out.) Focus your attention on working with the good stuff, stretching yourself and letting go of the rest. For example, if you've particular talent, look for ways to tell others about it and use it more. Begin delegating or changing the things people suggest you should do less of.

Feedback is an opinion. The point of feedback is to take what you can from it in the way that's right for you. Listen to it, take what supports you in building your confidence, and let the rest go.

Picturing the Life You'd Like to Lead

Confidence is almost all about perception. Very few people are wholly confident in every area of their life. Those who appear to be so are probably good actors.

Imagine having a PhD in Confidence. Think about how your life would be different if you had studied the subject, taken everything you discovered on board, and were supremely confident, firing on all cylinders.

Find yourself a quiet place to sit and contemplate for ten minutes. Picture yourself with your newfound super-confidence. Think of a real-life time coming up in your calendar where you'd like to be supremely confident in that 'I can conquer the world' quality. And start to notice . . .

- ✔ Where are you and who is with you?
- ✔ What are you doing?
- ✔ What skills and talents do you have now?
- ✔ What are your thoughts and feelings?
- ✔ What's really important to you about this newfound confidence?
- ✔ What would you do if you knew you couldn't fail?

Adjust the picture so that it feels right for you. Hold the picture for yourself and savour it so that you will be able to recall it whenever you want to.

Visualisation involves focusing your thoughts on the things you want to happen in your life and picturing them happening. Although it's a simple mental discipline, it can have dramatic effects. It's a powerful motivational tool that will help you take your confidence sky high.

Paying attention to what matters

As you become more confident, you start paying more attention to what's important to you rather than bowing to pressures from other people. By the time you've read this book, you'll know clearly what's important for you, and where you're going to choose to put your time and energy going forward.

Start now by answering one simple question: What really matters to you in your life right now? For example, do you want a loving partner or family around you, a successful career, or a better bill of health as your top priority? You may be working towards a highly specific goal such as running a marathon or planning the wedding of your dreams. Write your answer down and make it the priority for your confidence-building muscles.

Uncovering your confidence

Stay curious as to what kind of confident person you can be at your best. This question of who you can become is one that even the most experienced, capable chief executives and media personalities ask themselves regularly. Successful people stretch themselves constantly.

You've enormous potential limited only by yourself. And it's up to you to realise it. Gandhi had to overcome acute shyness to take on injustice in the world and free his people. And the more you connect with what is important to you, the more you become true to your most confident self.

People often feel a fraud when they take a new leadership role that's more senior. If you have this feeling, then remember that you've been selected for that important job because your company believes you will do it well. You're not being realistic to expect to have all the knowledge on day one. People invite you to join them because they know you can contribute, and they want you to grow and develop.

Not everyone wants or needs to be an international leader on the world stage, yet you can become a leader in your own world, inspiring others. Look back over time to things that you may take for granted. You've found out how to ride a bike or drive a car, to operate a computer, or renovate your house. As your skills and competence grow, so you become more confident to take on bigger challenges. Something that seemed hard five years ago may be a piece of cake today.

Be your own sponsor as well as critic. You may be good at giving yourself a hard time by comparing yourself unfavourably with other people: 'I'll never be as good as. . . .' Comparisons with others are valuable in that they can help you to excel and raise your game as a budding player on the golf circuit, for example. Don't waste energy beating yourself up by not being as good as the expert who dedicates every day of their life to practice.

You're important in this world and have a real contribution to make. Support, coaching, and personal sponsorship of various types will help you to be the very best you can be. Begin by assuming that you're going to be successful, and surround yourself with people who honour and support your growth.

So who are you really? The 'you' that you want to become is up to you, as you'll find out when you follow your own direction. In the words of Gandhi: 'You must be the change you wish to see in the world.'

Preparing for Action

There's no time like the present for getting started. Confidence starts here and now. Yes, that means today. Not on Monday morning after the excesses of the weekend.

Getting your confident self fired up means adopting a new, positive mind-set, and getting rid of any doubts you have. You'll get help with this mind-set in the next few chapters by cleaning up on your doubts. So before you set off on the journey, first check inside yourself. Ask yourself:

✔ Is it okay to make this change and become a more confident me?

✔ What do I stand to lose or gain if I do?

When you're happy that your answers are positive, even if it feels a bit scary, you're ready for the next step of the journey.

If a part of you is really unduly scared of change, it may be for a valid reason. Think about it, and if you're worried, check with your family or even a health professional such as doctor or counsellor about your physical and mental well-being.

Setting your intentions

As you set out on the journey, we want to state our intentions for you, and invite you to do the same. Our commitment is:

> We are committed to giving you our full support and sharing all our knowledge. We believe that you're a unique and special human being with your individual strengths. We also know that being kind and honest with yourself gives you the best results. We know that if you follow the tips and ideas in this book and put them into practice, you will build a more confident version of yourself to take out into the world.

Now, we ask that you make a declaration of your intent and speak it out loud to yourself three times with increasing commitment:

> I make a commitment to build my confidence in the way that's right for me, honouring myself as a unique and special human being. I will be honest with and kind to myself on the journey to be the very best I can be. I promise to have fun along the way.

Acknowledging the perils and perks of change

Any kind of change has its ups and downs. You can focus on the downside and say that you may be under threat from people who don't want a confident you, you may find changing scary, and you may put yourself on the line and open yourself up to criticism and sarcasm. So what? The power of change far outweighs the negatives. Look around and make your own judgement about who has the best life – confident people or shrinking violets. Confident people earn more money, have more fun, enjoy more freedom, and relish new experiences. They have a go, they discover, they've a zest for living. They love the power that comes from being confident to do the things that many other people shy away from.

A few tips then for riding the ups and downs as you change:

- ✓ **Flex your knees over the bumpy days.** Stay resolute and adapt your approach.

- ✓ **Look at the worst scenario.** Face up to it (it usually isn't that bad), and expect the best to happen. It usually does.

- ✓ **Ask yourself: What will this be like in a week's time, a month's time, or this time next year?** Taking a longer-term view usually strips away the anxiety.

Welcome on board the confidence train and happy travels!

Chapter 2

Identifying Your Sticking Points

● ●

In This Chapter

▶ Recognising when your natural confidence comes under attack

▶ Getting familiar with what pulls you down and holds you back

▶ Spotting new ways to break out of your inertia

● ●

*E*xuding confidence is a bit like being wealthy. Confidence, like money, only becomes a problem when it disappears. You've probably experienced times when you suddenly become aware of your confidence because you've lost it. You don't pay attention when confidence is coming at you in abundance and you've that pleasant, warm, 'can do' glow.

Now, we're not saying you should expect life to be 100 per cent perfect all the time. In fact, that's unrealistic. You can expect sticking points on any journey – times when your plans, hopes, and dreams don't run smoothly and you feel as if you're wading through treacle. The art of developing your confidence lies in minimising how long you let yourself stay mired in low-confidence land and how quickly you're able to let the causes go.

Getting on the road less boggy is what this chapter is all about. We show you how to face the tough times so that you can begin to let life flow for yourself. Rest assured that you may well encounter more tough times ahead – facing them is how you learn from life.

Soon you'll be ready to set your sights on your next destination, so for now, gather yourself together and prepare to jump down from the fence. It's time to get more decisive, make a commitment to change, and take responsibility for the results you get.

Digging Down to Root Issues

Cleaning up means digging deep to the heart of what really holds you back. You may not be fully aware of what gets in your way, but the clues are in what you say and how you describe your experience. Ever heard yourself utter things like 'It's *impossible* for me to leave my job', or 'I'm *always* going to have problems because I never went to the right school', or 'They'll *never* choose me for promotion because *everyone* knows they want someone who is younger/slimmer/ an accountant/a creative type/female/male/white/black, and so on.

Such statements are not based on reality, but on your perception of it. In fact, they're merely stories to frighten yourself with. These generalisations limit you and drain your confidence to have a go at whatever adventures lie ahead. They've the same negative effect on those around you.

The way you describe your world becomes your experience of it. As Einstein once famously pointed out: 'The most important question to ask, is: Is the universe a hostile or friendly place?' If you describe your world with hostile language, that is what you experience. Life becomes a nightmare if that's how you dream. Those who negatively distort reality suffer the most stress, anxiety, and depression, all of which get in the way of living confidently.

As you re-create your more confident reality, listen to your own words. Notice when your descriptions include words such as *always, never, everyone, nothing, totally, impossible.* Replace them or qualify them with more liberating words such as *I choose to, sometimes, possibly, almost.*

Forgetting the blame mind-set

You know who the whiners and blamers are around you. If you've any sense of personal protection, you steer well clear of them or limit your time with them. When you're stuck in blaming mode, positive people begin to avoid your company and you end up building friendships with those who reinforce your blame approach so that you can double up on your whingeing and whining.

The blame mind-set is not a helpful place to be if you want to get on and succeed in this world. Blame limits your choices and your results. You find fault in others rather than taking responsibility for the results you get. You wait around for others to do things before you act.

From our coaching conversations with business leaders and entrepreneurs, we can say for sure that they rarely hang around blaming others or making excuses: they do everything in their power to bring about change. They take it upon themselves to make a difference without expecting others to bale them out.

 This Parrot on Your Shoulder exercise can help you to shift your viewpoint and be more objective about your choices and your behaviour.

For one day, imagine that you're able to observe all your own behaviour – everything you do and say. You can be like a parrot on your own shoulder. Take notice when you think that a situation is due to what others around you are doing and when you make excuses for yourself. Then hear the parrot on your shoulder say: 'What are you *choosing* to do about it then?'

Getting past your past

As a lad of eight, John's secret dream was to be a ballet dancer, and he asked to audition for the school pantomime. When the school music teacher rejected him after a token interview, he overheard her say to a colleague: 'I could never have a fat boy like that in any production of mine.'

In spite of the teacher's unkind words, John went on to slim down and pursue his dream in *Billy Elliott* style. He had a highly successful international dance career before moving into the business world.

Your aim is to shift your blame mind-set into one in which you choose your outcome. Choosing your outcome transforms your world and opens up new possibilities. You switch your focus of attention from what has gone wrong to what you want to have happen instead. Two key indicators of confidence are self-awareness and flexibility in behaviour. With the imaginary parrot's help, you can raise your scores on both counts.

Rewriting your role in your family

Family relationships are dynamic, meaning that they change over time. Part of being confident is recognising that it's natural for you to have a different relationship with your parents, siblings, and the rest of the family as you grow older. Just because your big brother told you what to do when you were eight doesn't give him the right to behave in the same way 20 years on. Nor does it give you the excuse to slip into an unhelpful, child-like relationship with him.

 ANECDOTE

Being a child at 50

At the age of 50, Bruce appears to be a mature and confident man. He holds down a responsible lecturing job at a prestigious university and has published works of academic excellence. For most of the year, he is bright, entertaining, and fun to be with. But that all changes when his parents come to stay for Christmas.

Over the years, he has loved and lost a string of live-in girlfriends who despair at his change in behaviour when his mother and father visit. At these times, Bruce reverts to being a 'good little boy', trying to please his parents by adopting false modesty. Each time, the current girlfriend is ousted from the double bedroom and placed in a guest room, and treated as a casual visitor in the shared home. Bruce feels that his parents will not approve of the live-in relationship he has chosen and pretends that he lives a bachelor existence. He behaves as if he still lives in the parental home, and he lacks the emotional maturity to be his own person, not acknowledging the true situation for fear of upsetting his parents.

Little wonder, then, that many New Year parties have been less than romantic for Bruce.

Yet you may recognise that you cling to a pattern of behaviour with your family that's no longer appropriate to the confident you that you want to be today. You're also likely to play out these patterns at work or in other relationships, for example, biting your tongue when your needs aren't met, rather than saying what you feel is true and right.

You can choose how you want to be with people, and the way you behave dictates the results you get.

The next exercise helps you to shift the dynamics in your family relationships by observing the current situation, then choosing how you would like it to be. The exercise is hugely empowering, particularly if you feel stuck in old habits.

Think of a person in your family, including your in-laws or step children, who you'd like to relate to in a better way. Follow these steps:

1. **Write out the story of how you currently relate to this person.**

   Describe how you currently behave with this person. Note the situations that you find most difficult and challenging. Think about what you would like to change so that you can have a respectful, amicable, and mature relationship with this person.

2. **Write a second version detailing how you would like this relationship to be in three years' time.**

   Write in the present tense as if the change has already happened. Add as much detail as you like to visualise the new story with dialogue and your new feelings.

3. **Act as if you've already developed or changed this relationship.**

   Make a commitment to yourself that next time you have contact with this person, you will remind yourself of your new story. Visualising the future, behave as if the change you desire has already happened.

Benefiting from your life experiences

Sam gave up his job in computer sales to teach yoga full time. He has that almost tangible inner strength of so many yogis and martial artists – a highly centred kind of energy. One day at the end of a class, he commented that after fleeing from atrocities in Uganda at the age of 15 nothing fazes him. He left his family and was sent off to Canada alone to meet up with one family contact, who helped him to find a room to live in. Subsequently, he suffered a number of setbacks in life from which he bounced back.

In a bizarre way, the awful times you come through provide the root source for your strongest confidence. They build your resilience and toughen you up to face the next hurdle.

Table 2-1 provides room for you to list some of the tough times you've faced in your life so far and how dealing with them benefited you. Your own tough times don't need to be as extreme as Sam's.

Table 2-1	Your Tough Times Index		
Tough Time	*Obstacles Overcome*	*Benefits*	*How to Put Benefits to Use*
Sam's example: Expulsion from home country	Separation from family	Self-confidence	Take risks with new ventures
	Financial hardship	Resilience	Follow personal dreams
		Independence	
Your example: 1			
Your example: 2			
Your example: 3			

Cleaning Out the Negatives

It's spring-cleaning time – time to get started on some broad-brush clean-up action. Begin by facing up to some of that negative, confidence-draining stuff. Our belief is that you were born confident, and somehow along the way you let people and circumstances get in your way.

Working or living in a mess wipes your energy. Just to get you in the clean-up/feel-good mood, take 15 minutes right now for a tidy-up. If you're at work, make it a desk sweep. Clear the decks, put your desk in order. If you're at home, take the space in the house where you spend the most time, and make it as attractive as you can for yourself right now. Already obsessively tidy? Then pat yourself on the back for being so organised, and lie back and relax for ten minutes.

Designing and creating your own life, as the next sections help you to do, is much more fun than spending all your energy constantly troubleshooting and problem solving.

Tackling unhelpful assumptions

You may be holding on to unhelpful thoughts or assumptions about yourself – most people do – that prevent you from feeling fully confident. Perhaps you think that life or work has to be a huge effort and an uphill struggle all the way. Maybe you compare yourself unfavourably with other people.

Some of the assumptions we hear as coaches include:

- ✔ 'I'm not a confident person because I left school at 15.'
- ✔ 'It's easy for you to be confident at work because you have marketable skills.'
- ✔ 'I won't be confident until I can work part-time.'
- ✔ 'He comes from money, so he's bound to be confident.'
- ✔ 'I'll feel confident when I've lost my excess weight.'
- ✔ 'I'm not part of the elite crowd, so it's no surprise I lack confidence.'

These comments are loaded with judgement and unfavourable comparisons with others rather than fact. The trouble with taking on such unhelpful assumptions is that you act as if the assumption is true until it becomes a self-fulfilling prophecy.

Take a few moments to record some unhelpful assumptions about your own confidence that hold you back. Then write down an opposing, more positive assumption. For example, an unhelpful statement goes like this: 'Since I've turned 40, I can't ever expect to feel confident going on a date.' Turning that around produces the more powerful: 'Now I'm 40, I can ask anyone out for a date with supreme confidence.'

Remind yourself of your new assumptions regularly. An easy way is to write them out on a small card and place it on your desk or bathroom mirror where you can see it every day.

There may be an element of good fortune in any activity, but the more you practise, the luckier you get . . . as all top performers will tell you.

Staying busy but not overwhelmed

If you love life, you may well work to an action-packed schedule: So many people to see, so many things to do. To function at your truly confident best, strike a balance between busy time and rest time. If you're constantly on the run, you start to feel off-balance, which eventually topples your internal sense of confidence.

Busyness does not equal effectiveness.

Recognising signals that you're at your limits

The following clues indicate that you're in danger of being overwhelmed:

- ✔ You run late for appointments or miss them altogether.

- ✔ You forget what you were doing.

- ✔ You get easily distracted and start many projects without finishing any of them.

- ✔ You lose things like your keys, your mobile phone, and the shopping list.

✔ Your house or office paperwork is chaotic.

✔ You feel jittery inside.

✔ You snap at people you care about.

✔ You stop listening to other people.

✔ Your eating habits are poor – you eat late at night or grab sandwiches from the local garage.

✔ You let people down on commitments.

✔ You catch sight of yourself in a mirror and look like a frightened rabbit.

If more than two or three of these clues sound like you, congratulations. You've recognised some of the signals of being overwhelmed and this is the first step necessary to making change.

Using the four Ps to take stock

If you feel that you've got too much to do and too little time to do it all, realise that you're not alone. Then realise that you can do something about it.

The best way to cut out whatever is getting in your way is to stop and take stock – ideally at the start of each day. Follow these steps to assign a priority to each task on your to-do list:

1. **Draw up a list of everything you want to accomplish today.**

   (If you're well organised, you will have done that last night.)

2. **Colour code each item on the list.**

   • Red for **panics and problems:** The important, deadline-driven jobs you want to resolve quickly which fit with your priorities.

   • Green indicates **plans and opportunities:** The important, longer-term activities you'd like to spend time on. Include recreation as well as larger projects.

   • Blue for **pressing items:** The things other people are pushing you to do, but which are not top of your to-do list for today.

- Yellow indicates **pootling issues:** The chats with friends and more trivial timewasters during which you drift around aimlessly.

Your aim is to make the plans and opportunities list – the green one – largest of all and to reduce the size of the others. This area is most important because it enables you to put your energy on what's most important to you and save you getting stressed by deadlines, or just drift around listlessly.

3. **Allocate your time today so that you can clear up some problems from your red list, build in space for the plans and opportunities in your green list, and see how much of the pressing (blue) and pootling (yellow) items you can cut out.**

Become aware of what type of activities dominate your schedule most of the time. The colour coding is a quick visual guide to your effectiveness.

Redirecting those inner voices

Juliet came to a coaching session with Kate when she took on a senior project management role that required her to host international conference calls, manage a new team, and chair committee meetings. She knew logically that she was capable of the role and that she had the full support of the Senior Management Team, yet she experienced crises of confidence at unexpected times. Through coaching, she identified a number of voices running in her head that we named and shamed as 'gremlins'. One was the 'You should be seen and not heard' gremlin. Another was the 'Hurry up, don't waste time' gremlin. Under stress, these gremlins undermined Juliet's confidence. Over a period of months, these gremlins fell back into the shadows as she paid more attention to the voices that told her, 'You deserve to be heard, loud and clear', and 'Allow yourself the time it takes to do your best job without being hurried.'

What about your own inner voices? What do you say to yourself about yourself? What are those inner voices, running in your head? As coaches, we often hear limiting fears that pop up for clients such as: 'Who do you think you are to take on this challenge? You'll get found out soon enough. You're a fraud. Are you good enough? Don't you think you should know your place? You're not a confident person, so what are you doing here?'

How can you tame these voices? In many creative ways, once you put your mind to it.

✔ Picture the friendly parrot on your shoulder (who flew in to the 'Getting past the blame mind-set' section earlier in this chapter) programmed with a positive message to repeat every time it hears a negative thought: 'I was chosen because I'm the best.' 'I can do this.' 'I am good enough.' 'I'm going to show you just how good I really am.'

✔ Imagine the negative voices playing on your stereo, then turning the volume control down to a hushed whisper, and finally gently flicking the off switch. Imagine deleting the music file or cutting up the CD.

✔ Look for the positive intention of the negative voice. Figure out how this voice is trying to help you. Acknowledge it, thank it, and tell it to go away now that it's served a useful purpose.

You *can* clear out those unwanted messages.

Discovering What Drains Your Batteries

Confident people bounce with positive, focused energy – they're happy with themselves and life – and they're infectious to be with. They've clarity in their direction. Less confident people can drain the energy from everyone around them. Spend time with them and you're left feeling tired and exhausted. Ideally, you don't have many of what we call *toxic friends* because you wipe them out, park them elsewhere, or neutralise them before they wipe you out.

Then you have *toxic situations* – times and places that are just not right for you. In the following sections we invite you to line up all those damaging elements you're sticking with, and make the decision that you're no longer going to put up with them. You can get them out of your system once and for all. Freedom beckons!

Counting the cost of toleration

When we first met Julie, she was unhappy and exhausted at work, which resulted in a loss of confidence in her own technical skills. She had been off sick suffering from stress and depression, feeling unsupported in her job of delivering to tight deadlines for government projects. Her colleagues put more and more load onto Julie, who was conscientious about meeting deadlines, however unrealistic. Her energy was increasingly sapped in this toxic environment until she discovered how to push back the load and protect herself.

Now it's time to stop and consider what you may be tolerating that is gradually sapping your confidence. Table 2-2 gives you space to rate common confidence sappers according to how often you experience them. Go through the list in the table and mark the appropriate box for each item.

Table 2-2	Rating Confidence Sappers			
Sapper	*Rating*			
Work	**Never**	**Occasionally**	**Frequently**	**Always**
Overstretched/ long hours				
Talents unused				
Insufficient training				
Unfair pay or reward				
Bullying				
Lack of support from boss				
Poor working conditions/tools				
Home and social				
Unfair allocation of chores				
Financial insecurity				

Sapper	Rating			
Home and social	**Never**	**Occasionally**	**Frequently**	**Always**
Unattractive/ untidy house				
Unpleasant behaviour/ negativity				
Excessive noise				
Lack of quality time				
Toxic friends who are demanding				
Poor health				
Lack of exercise				

Now group your answers and rank them in order of their ability to sap your energy with the worst at the top.

- ✔ What is your number one confidence sapper, the thing that drains your energy the most?

- ✔ What is the effect on you of tolerating this?

    For example: Is it making you ill? Is it upsetting your relationships with other people? Is it costing you money?

- ✔ If you solved this one, what would be the bigger benefit in your life?

    For example: If you cleared the clutter in your house, could you invite a new boyfriend/girlfriend over for a romantic evening?

- ✔ What is your first step in dealing with this?

    Beyond your larger plan, think of something you can do to reach your goal *today*. Even if you only take one tiny step forward, do something *now*.

You don't have to struggle on your own. Engage the help of an independent coach who has only your interests at heart.

Trying to meet everyone's needs except your own

Busy people have a tendency to take on more and more because they see what needs doing and know how to get things done. Recognise the pattern?

You may be tempted to chase around the world helping everyone else except yourself. Doing so, however, can drain your energy in a drip-feed kind of way until you stop noticing it. You run around so much after other people, and dissipate your energy with your concerns about them, that you forget to look after yourself too.

As you begin to recognise more about where you are stuck in the confidence stakes and what holds you back, one particularly important question for you to consider is: *How do you know when your needs are being met?*

To answer this question, look at your life and see whether you sleep well each night; eat wholesome food; develop enriching relationships; enjoy your work; and have time for hobbies, time out, and exercise. If not, then the balance may have tipped too much in favour of supporting others.

At the end of the day, do a final check to make sure that you've done something good for yourself today, as well as supporting everyone else. If not, then put it top of your agenda for tomorrow.

The most confident people are generous to others and to themselves at the same time. They've high self-esteem – they know that they must value themselves and their time as well as that of others.

Chapter 3

Charting Your Course Ahead

*B*uilding anything is bound to be more difficult without specific information on what you're trying to build. In this chapter, you look in more detail at the more confident you that you want to build and define the actions you want to take.

Knowing Where You Want to Go

Many self-help books explain a variety of powerful techniques to help you reach your goals. These methods range from the highly practical tools used by professional project managers to the more gentle and esoteric methods of planting visions and feelings onto your future timeline and in your subconscious. These techniques all have one thing in common: you have to know what you want to accomplish or where you want to get to.

Does this ring any bells with you? You may be surprised at how often people feel that they need to strive to get somewhere really important with no clear notion of where they're going. You know that you want to bring something into your life, but you haven't yet discovered exactly what it is. You've more of a feeling of dissatisfaction with the status quo, or a sense of knowing that you're capable of so much more.

Gaining a clear sense of where you're trying to get to, and why that destination is important to you, is absolutely critical in achieving your dreams and becoming confident in the world.

Determining your areas of focus

A useful tool you can use to home in on areas you want to address is the *confidence wheel,* which is widely used by business and life coaches around the world. Figure 3-1 shows a sample wheel (you decide your own categories and scores – we just give examples here).

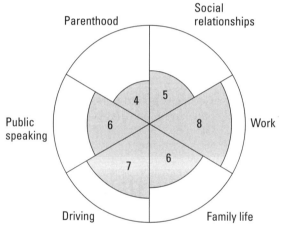

Figure 3-1: Spinning a confidence wheel.

To make your own confidence wheel, follow these steps:

1. **Make a list of the areas of your life in which your confidence plays an important part.**

   Your list should include such things as social relationships, work, family life, and so on.

   You can have as many or as few as you like but six or eight is usually a good number to start with. These become the specific areas you work on to increase your all round self-confidence.

2. **Give yourself a score out of 10 in each area, in which 10 represents the level of confidence you would like to feel.**

This score represents how confident you generally feel compared with how confident you would like to feel. For example, you may feel generally confident in your job and give yourself 8/10 for that, but perhaps you feel less confident in your social life and you score this category at only 4/10.

3. **Draw a large circle on a sheet of plain paper and divide it into the same number of segments as you have items on your list. Label each segment to represent each area of your life in which you want to develop more confidence.**

4. **Draw a line in each segment to represent the score you gave yourself in Step 2.**

   If you score a segment 5/10, draw the line halfway between the centre of the segment and its edge. You don't have to be completely accurate; the idea is to create a visual representation of your confidence in the more important aspects of your life.

The confidence wheel you generate gives you a comparative assessment of the areas of your life in which you feel most and least confident. You can use it to create more balance in your life and to show you the areas that you'd benefit most from working on. This information is useful in goal setting, and also in understanding how it feels when you're more or less confident facing any new situation.

Taken in the round, your wheel also gives you an indication of the degree of balance or imbalance in your confidence in various aspects of your life. If this wheel were the wheel on a real vehicle, how bumpy a ride would you be getting? This exercise gives you a useful insight into prioritising the areas you may want to address first. With this knowledge, you can draw a map to your destination; without it, you are guaranteed to fail.

Mapping your own journey

By flipping ahead to Chapter 5, you can gain a deepening understanding of your values and sense of purpose. For now, identifying just a few well-defined areas that you'd like to change or improve while your deeper sense of purpose is emerging is enough.

A popular and easy-to-use system for making change happen is the *SMART model*, where you address the aspect that each letter stands for in sequence. To get started with the SMART model, think of something you want to bring into your life right now and write down your answers as you work through the following list:

- ✔ **S** stands for **specific.** Define what you want to achieve as specifically as possible. If you want a car, decide on the make, the model, the colour, trim, year, and the price you're prepared to pay. Find a picture or two of the *specific* car you want and pin them up in strategic places where you see them every day. The more specific you are, the more effective your goal-achieving behaviour becomes.

- ✔ **M** stands for **measurable.** With an object such as a car, measuring your achievement is easy – you have it or you don't. Your progress towards some goals, though, is more difficult to measure. Say your objective is to be more present with your family. First you must decide what this objective means *specifically* (the amount of time you spend at home, how long you focus on your partner's conversation, and so on) and then you can set up your equally specific *measures.* And don't forget to write them down.

- ✔ **A** stands for **attainable.** The trick here is to make your goal a challenge and a stretch without it being overwhelming. Athletes are good at this trick. They constantly set themselves new challenges, personal bests, and so on, pushing on their performance standards to new heights in challenging chunks. You can set intermediate goals if necessary to keep yourself moving in the right direction.

- ✔ **R** stands for **rewarding.** Asking yourself regularly why you want to achieve a particular goal and linking this to your growing confidence about who you're being in the world and what you're doing with your time are absolutely critical – and often get forgotten. Having the *why* written down and available in your moments of weakness provides you with the motivation to carry on, to get through this tough patch, and to move on towards your goal. The bigger the reward, the stronger your motivation. With a big enough 'why', you never give up.

✔ T stands for **time.** Having a deadline can be motivating. It keeps you focused on achievement against plan and allows you to set up milestones for your bigger, more complicated goals. If your goal is to achieve your ideal weight by Christmas, then December 25 becomes your deadline, and you can work backwards from then to set yourself a series of intermediate goals.

Your increasing insights into how to set goals and achieve the things you want in life are an enormous support to your growing confidence. You can never know what is around the next corner, but you can rely on your growing skills and understanding to get you through it. Onwards and upwards!

When you're at your most powerful and confident, the things you take on in the world, the way you behave, your skills, experiences, and competencies, what is important to you, your beliefs, your sense of who you are and what you are here to do are all of a piece – making you, in personal development terms, congruent or aligned.

Setting milestones along the way

A good technique for broad-brush, big-picture goal setting is to think about how you want things to be in your healthy old age. Choose an age, say 85, and picture yourself at the centre of your network of family and friends doing whatever you want to be doing at that age. Focus on what you're doing, how fit and healthy you are, what your weight is, how you occupy your time, and what you enjoy doing.

Now figure out what you need to be like at 65 to make this life possible, and at 50, and so on. By thinking backwards, you can add layer after layer of detail, as much as you want to give yourself a much clearer sense of what you need to make happen over the next five to ten years to give you the life you want.

Following the Guaranteed Success Formula

Many versions of the *Guaranteed Success Formula* exist, and they all essentially tackle the problem of getting the result you want. You can use this simple six-step version straight away:

1. **Decide what you want.**

2. **Plan what you need to do to get what you want.**

3. **Take the necessary action.**

   (Confidence comes into it here.)

4. **Notice what result you're getting.**

5. **Vary your action in light of your results.**

6. **Repeat Steps 2 to 5 until you get the result you want.**

Perhaps the most-cited example of the benefits of following this formula is Thomas Edison, the American inventor and entrepreneur, who is credited with having found 9,999 ways of *not* inventing the light bulb before getting it right.

A more up-to-date and less apocryphal example is how computers effortlessly achieve complex mathematical estimations. They sometimes perform millions of mathematical operations in just a few seconds using the Guaranteed Success Formula before presenting you with the optimal answer to the problem, using the Guaranteed Success Formula to get the correct result. (Chapter 12 explores the formula in more detail.)

Alcoholics Anonymous operates a highly successful personal development programme that literally saves lives. One of its teachings is that acting your way into a new way of thinking is easier than thinking your way into a new way of acting. Go on, change some of your behaviours and be sensitive to how people begin to behave differently to you.

Choosing Role Models

One way of speeding up the trial and error element of the Guaranteed Success Formula is to find an example of someone doing something the way you would like to and emulating, or *modelling,* not just what they're doing but also how they're doing it (including, as much as you can, what they're actually thinking and feeling while they're doing it).

Autobiographies provide a good source of insight into how prominent people have approached the achievements for which they're noted and how they developed their own confidence. In his autobiography, *Small Man in a Book*, for example, the actor and comedian Rob Brydon writes about his years of toil on stage before achieving a breakthrough with some beautifully crafted comedies to launch his showbiz career. The book is about how he struggled and kept going in the face of failure, a journey that he describes as 'a story of triumph over adversity'. When his comedy *Marion and Geoff* (which featured monologues from a lonely, divorced taxi driver) received critical acclaim, he began winning awards. Looking back at that time, Rob says 'I finally found my voice and was putting out work that was personal to me'.

Finding reliable guides

Ask yourself who you most admire, and why. If you want to be more like that person, find out what you can about how they approach the things you would like to emulate and use this knowledge to inform your own application of the Guaranteed Success Formula. The more precise and specific you can be about this knowledge, the better.

ANECDOTE

Enriching her life with theirs

Tanya is an avid reader of autobiographies and she finds them an enduring source of inspiration in her life of caring for her partner, children, and elderly parents while her career is on hold.

She loves the personal accounts of triumph over adversity such as that of Lance Armstrong, who beat cancer to set world records in cycle racing at the Tour de France and the Irish tenor and recording artist Ronan Tynan, who also set world athletic records after being born with defects that meant his legs and feet never fully developed. Equally, she loves to read about those who set and achieve 'impossible' targets, like Sir Steve Redgrave, who won rowing gold medals at five separate Olympic games over a 20-year career at the very pinnacle of athletic performance.

Most of all, though, she loves to read about the awakening of the spirit, such as happened with the beautiful Queen Noor of Jordan who, as Lisa Halaby an American architect planner, met and married King Hussein and became an inspirational focus for the interests of women and children, education, arts, and culture in the Arab world.

In the first-hand accounts of all these true lives, Tanya finds the comfort, knowledge, and inspiration to keep her own standards high and her own performance on track for the life of her choosing. When she eventually restarts her career, she – bring a new depth and wisdom to her work based on the high standards and values evident in the great lives she has been steadily absorbing.

Keep in mind that even true heroes have feet of clay – we all do. What you should care most about is how someone has achieved a standard of performance or developed a character trait that you want to emulate. Focus on the sporting excellence rather than the womanising, or the artistic brilliance rather than the drug abuse. Don't fall prey to the *halo effect* that occurs when you set your heroes on pedestals, then watch in horrid fascination when the tabloid newspapers and scandal sheets expose their faults and failings.

A useful metaphor is that of Steve Austin in the old television show *The Six Million Dollar Man*. After he was severely damaged in a near-fatal accident, scientists rebuilt Steve to be far faster, stronger, and all-round better than he was originally. You may want to run like Michael Johnson, be funny like Jerry Seinfeld, or score goals like Pelé. Whatever does it for you, be specific.

Becoming your own coach

You've the opportunity of becoming your own coach as you grow in understanding and knowledge of how to get the best out of yourself. Becoming your own coach isn't as difficult as it may seem at first and you can make a start with just a few pointers.

Think about the attributes of a coach. Coaches take a dispassionate view of the client's performance. They look carefully to consider what is actually happening before making suggestions for change or improvement. Coaches see it and tell it like it is: no better, no worse.

Seeing it and telling it like it is, is a useful skill that you can easily develop with just a little practice. Start right now. Stop for a moment and imagine yourself across the room observing the real you that is reading this book. Describe the scene in simple, clear, unambiguous phrases like: 'She is sitting and reading the text, she puts the book down periodically and appears to be thinking about something, occasionally she writes a note in the margin.'

Coaches tend to use simple, direct language in telling it like it is. They make no value judgements, and serve up none of the 'She seems to be daydreaming again, she seems unable to concentrate on anything for more than a few minutes; there she goes again, she'll never get this done' or any of the other things you may habitually say to yourself. When *you* are being the coach, you first need to look and consider what is really happening, and only then think constructively about how best to move the performance or situation forward.

Becoming the hero in your own life

One of the most effective ways of raising your performance in anything is to 'raise your game'; that is, raising your expectations and your personal standards. Who is the real hero of your life? You are, of course, and your standard of performance will be more influential than anything else in shaping the life you experience.

Most people think of a hero as someone who is born with an exceptional character, courage, and bravery. Perhaps the hero has some externally imposed goal, such as the restoration of his birthright after a usurper stole his father's crown (think of Simba in *The Lion King*).

Real life isn't like this, of course, but that doesn't mean that no heroes exist in real life. Shakespeare reminds us that some are born great, some achieve greatness, and some have greatness thrust upon them. And this saying applies equally to women and men, even though the classical heroes are usually male.

So what does a real-life hero look like? Take a look in the mirror. Yes, a real-life hero looks a lot like you, right here, right now. Every life is a rerun of the classical hero's journey you read about as a child, and every one of us in our own way faces the hero's choices of good over evil, light over dark, right over wrong, and going forwards into growth or shrinking backwards into fear.

To become the hero in the story of your life, follow these steps:

1. **Decide that you're going to take on personal change to enable you to achieve the things you want in life, and get into action.**

Be kind and supportive to yourself. You aren't going to get things right first time, so expect setbacks and think about how you can manage and recover from them. Determine how to get yourself back on track efficiently.

2. **Decide where you're going, or what you really want.**

   Set your SMART goals using the techniques we outlined earlier in this chapter. Some goals can be relatively short term and fun, whereas others may be more serious and take you many years to accomplish. Reach for the stars: your journey – last your lifetime and you don't want to complete it too soon.

3. **Plan your work and work your plan.**

   You always accomplish more – and more quickly and reliably – when you have a plan. The plan itself is of limited use if you don't work it. Vary it, change it, but stick with it. Your plan is your friend – and a hero needs a reliable friend.

4. **Don't compete, create!**

   Don't view your life as a competition and the people you meet along the way as your competitors. On heroes' journeys, other people appear as messengers, allies, and resources. Sometimes they bring you warnings; other times they bring you keys and answers to the questions you're posing. Only rarely do you meet an enemy outside yourself – your enemy is most often found in the gremlins within you, holding you back, and you need to be creative to outsmart them.

5. **Pay attention to your lessons before you apply them.**

   Hear the truths that strangers bring to you before you try to drown them out with your own truth and enthusiasm for your journey. Life tends to repeat the lessons you don't pick up on first time, so be alert and embrace what life shows you.

6. **Care for your companions on the journey.**

   As Shakespeare also said, the world is a stage and we all must play a part. You've changed your part to put yourself at the centre of your own heroic epic, but you need other characters to give your epic richness and colour. You don't want to end up a lonely old king living alone in your magnificent castle of dreams. Be kind to those whose journeys interact with yours.

7. **Listen to your inner coach.**

   Your inner coach knows you and knows what you need. Don't neglect your daily needs in pursuit of your future.

As you gain new and powerful insights into what you do, why you do things this way, and the choices you are making, you become more aware of your true potential. This awakening is an essential step on every hero's journey.

If you take on this way of being, you'll be amazed by the change you bring into your life. And when you take on a professional coach to help you, you can make faster progress through having found out how to be coachable.

If the idea of your personal hero's journey intrigues you, you can find other tools online at www.yourmostconfident self.com – the authors' website.

Part II
Gathering the Elements

The 5th Wave   By Rich Tennant

"I'm looking for someone who will love me for who I think I am."

In this part . . .

You find out how to take action when your motivation is challenged. You're invited to connect with the ideals and goals that drive you. You gain a better understanding of the deepest values at the core of your most confident actions. You delve into emotional stuff as you learn to live with your mood swings – both the highs and lows. Really importantly, you uncover your true passions so that you stop sitting on the sidelines and realise your dreams.

Chapter 4

Finding Your Motivation

● ●

In This Chapter

▶ Understanding motivation and how it links to confidence

▶ Applying motivation theories to increase your confidence

● ●

*Y*our personal motivation is the force that gets you out of bed in the morning and provides you with energy for the work of the day. This motivation is what keeps you pressing forward in the face of difficulties. Have you ever wondered why you seem to be bursting with it some days, and other times it seems to desert you entirely?

Understanding how motivation works so that you can access your natural motivation to help manage the life you want with more confidence and ease is what this chapter is about. It gives you the insight you need to keep moving forward despite the challenges you face.

The most important thing you can take from this chapter is that you don't have to put up with feeling weak and unmotivated, lacking in confidence. If you deal intelligently with blocks in your natural energy source, you can restore your energy, achieve more with less effort, and feel more at ease with life, more satisfied with yourself, and more confident and powerful in the world.

Driving Forward in Your Life

The more motivated you feel, the more inclined you are to push yourself through the things that are holding you back, (which is how we define confidence in Chapter 1). If you can increase your motivation, you automatically increase your confidence. In the next sections, we look at Abraham

Maslow's influential hierarchy of needs to help you gain insight into what motivates you and everyone you come into contact with.

Rising through Maslow's hierarchy of needs

One of the founders of the human potential movement, Abraham Maslow, is best known for his work on human motivation. He was fascinated by what makes some people able to face huge challenges in life, and especially what makes them refuse to give up despite incredible odds. He developed the model for which he is best known – his hierarchy of needs, shown in Figure 4-1 – to explain the forces that motivate people.

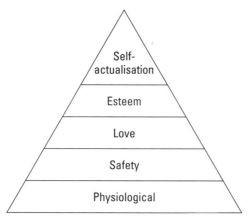

Figure 4-1: Looking at Maslow's hierarchy of needs.

Maslow saw men and women being constantly drawn on through life by the irresistible pull of unsatisfied needs. He grouped human needs into a hierarchy, which everyone shares and needs to satisfy from the bottom up. This model is widely taught in management development courses, but his work goes far beyond the workplace to the very heart of our humanity.

Maslow believed that you must first satisfy your basic physiological needs for air, water, food, sleep, and so on before any other desires will surface. As a member of modern society, these basic needs are largely taken care of for you, but if you've ever been short of breath under water you know and understand how this first-tier, physiological need dominates everything else until satisfied.

But when your physiological needs are met, you automatically shift up to the next level in the hierarchy to your broader need for safety – and that now drives you. Again, modern society tends to provide safe environments, but whenever you do feel threatened, you experience an automatic anxiety response and cannot think of much else until the situation is resolved and you feel safe again.

At the next level, you have to make more personal interventions to ensure that your needs are satisfied within the framework that society provides for you. Your needs for love and connection show up here; things you don't automatically get all the time. If your needs at this level are unsatisfied, and you feel isolated or lonely, you find it almost impossible to meet your higher-level needs in any meaningful way.

The next level is where your needs for self-esteem and recognition kick in. These needs may never have been an issue for you as you struggled to join your group, but now they can become dominant. It is no longer enough simply to belong; now you must have some power and status in the group too – drive a bigger car, become captain of the golf club perhaps, or chair of the school parent–teacher association. This level is where most established adults reside most of the time today.

But thankfully, the endless striving does end, and with all your needs taken care of, you eventually arrive at the top of Maslow's hierarchy as a fully developed human being. At the exotically named *self-actualisation* stage, your major motivation becomes living and expressing what is truly most important to you in life. Often, this stage is where you get to give something back to the world that has supported you so royally in your journey through life so far.

Maslow's hierarchy of needs helps to explain so much of the variability in human behaviour. Different human beings operate at different levels, and are driven by different needs at any given time. Your motivation level may be different on Monday from on Friday with the weekend looming. And of course, you may feel different at work from the way you feel at home. The more you understand what drives you, the better able you are to find the confidence to achieve the things you want in life.

Greeting the world with grace

Maslow is often associated with motivation at work, but his insights apply equally in social situations where you can use them to help put yourself at ease.

When you find yourself in a new social group – meeting new people at a party or function, for example – you can expect to feel anxious because *at this moment* you're at Maslow's third level, needing to be accepted into this new group.

You can still meet and greet people confidently, of course, but you may not feel like it right now. When you're in this situation, the first thing to do is to accept your mild anxiety about it. Nothing is wrong with feeling nervous (in case the voice inside your head starts accusing you of being a wimp), but you don't need to let these feelings prevent you from making new friends.

Remember, everyone in the room fits into Maslow's hierarchy and is therefore feeling needy at some level. The people you're meeting who are not new to the group are operating at the second and third levels: some are still anxious for acceptance, just as you are (and these people are just as keen to be accepted by you as you are by them); some are motivated by their need for social esteem and need your respect.

Depending on the kind of party you're at, you can expect to witness needy behaviours at all levels from hunger and thirst, through sex, connection, companionship, to a close approximation of self-actualisation on the dance floor. Don't judge your fellow partygoers too harshly. In fact, give everyone at the party a break, including you. Enjoy the spectacle!

Take on board these new factors in an otherwise ordinary and potentially dull social dynamic by paying attention to the curious and interesting display of need-motivated behaviours going on around you.

ANECDOTE

Beyond shyness into phobia

Neil had been an extremely shy and reserved person from early adolescence. And while everyone feels nervous in social situations from time to time, Neil's nervousness was not the normal kind but magnified on frequent occasions into disproportionate fear and anxiety, which totally sapped his confidence.

His symptoms were intense with persistent fears of situations where he didn't know people and where he felt they would be judging him. These fears led him to avoid these situations to a degree that affected his social life and work. Even so, he still feared being embarrassed or humiliated and was particularly sensitive that others would notice him blushing, sweating, and sometimes even shaking. He was finally able to recognise that his problem was more than just shyness, and that his fears were excessive and unreasonable for the situations he faced.

Neil found out that when social anxieties become extreme and disrupt your life, they may have crossed the line into a medical condition known as social phobia, or *social anxiety disorder*. He checked into the symptoms on the Internet and was worried enough to seek medical help.

In Neil's case, the diagnosis was *global social phobia*, a condition that affects virtually all social situations and so can be easily confused

with shyness. He was told that it can lead to substance abuse, alcoholism, depression, and even suicide, but that treatment was readily available.

His treatment was a combination of drugs to help balance his seratonin levels (seratonin is a hormone that helps keep moods under control by helping with sleep, calming anxiety, and relieving depression) and cognitive behaviour therapy based on the premise that it was Neil's own thoughts, rather than the situations he was facing, that were causing his extreme reaction.

Around 5 per cent of the readers of this book are likely to suffer from social phobia and yet soldier on in private, sometimes for years, avoiding and suffering in social situations. Only when they accept, like Neil, that they need medical assistance does it become possible to diagnose their condition and begin a course of treatment. The effects of medical intervention can often be liberating and profound, opening the door to a much more fulfilling and rewarding life.

Neil's seratonin is more stable now and he may soon be able to discontinue the drugs. The therapy has helped him to think in a different way, just like the ideas in this book will help you to think in a more positive and helpful way, increasing your confidence in many situations.

If you're curious about the people in the group and really take an interest in what's happening, you come across to others as attentive and a great conversationalist. This situation is more fun for you, and more fun for the people you meet. Pretty soon, everyone will want you at their parties.

Bringing this more curious and attentive version of yourself into social situations lessens your anxiety, because you focus on the impression other people are making on you rather than the one you're making on them. You always appear charming to those you meet if you give them the gift of your rapt attention. People aren't used to this attention and they'll love you for it.

Taking Charge at Work

Your ability to take action (our definition of confidence) is critical to your performance in the world, and in work this ability is usually just as important to the performance of your boss and co-workers too. For this reason, motivation for action has become the focus of a lot of social science research over the last 60 years, and in this section, we show you how to use some of this research for your personal benefit at work.

Looking at usable theory

Maslow's theory about human needs is universal, applying to everyone in all situations. Other important theorists, such as Frederick Herzberg and William McGregor, have focused on your motivation to achieve results at work, which is important to you and to your employer. In this section, you find out how to take more control of and increase your motivation at work. You also find a self-test to help you to measure your progress.

Searching for satisfaction with Herzberg

Frederick Herzberg is a motivation guru frequently studied on management development courses (which means that your senior colleagues should have heard about him). His elegant theory reveals the factors that energise you at work, helping you to behave confidently and get things done, and those that take your natural energy away. He separates out those forces that motivate people, called *motivators*, from those that sap motivation, the *dissatisfiers*. He discovered that these forces operate in a surprising, seemingly illogical way.

Take pay as a universal example. You may think that the money you're paid provides you with motivation, and most employers act as though money is the main motivation, but it simply isn't true in the long term according to Herzberg. Pay is a dissatisfier and not a motivator. If you aren't being paid the rate for the job, your poor pay rate can certainly make you feel dissatisfied, but surprisingly, of itself being paid over the odds doesn't motivate you any further than being paid a fair rate (although it may bring other factors into play, such as recognition and team status).

Recognition, on the other hand, is a motivator. For this reason, a good job title, a sincere word of thanks from the boss, or a mention in the in-house journal for a job well done can be so motivating.

Table 4-1 contains a list of some of the main motivators and dissatisfiers that Herzberg identified. The dissatisfiers on the left have to be carefully managed or they can create serious dissatisfaction for you, but of themselves they cannot motivate you. The factors on the right are the motivators and give you the drive you need to feel confident and do your best work, but they don't come into play until the dissatisfiers have first been neutralised.

Table 4-1 Factors Affecting Job Attitudes

Dissatisfiers	Motivators
Company policies	Achievement
Style of supervision	Recognition
Relationship with boss	Work itself
Working conditions	Responsibility
Salary	Advancement
Relationship with peers	Personal growth

Notice that the factors in the left column are external to the work itself and are largely imposed on you from outside. The motivators in the satisfaction column are much more personal, in that they tend to be more closely tied to the job you do. They're also more psychological, in that you've personal discretion over how much of them you feel. For this reason, you can use them to maintain your confidence levels.

If this insight starts to resonate powerfully for you, you may want to read up a bit more on Herzberg's motivation-hygiene theory before having a discussion about it with your boss. The dissatisfiers present in your work may be easy for your boss to neutralise, leaving you unencumbered psychologically to bring your motivation into play.

Unless you feel the presence of the motivators to a degree that has significance for you, you won't be motivated or satisfied at work no matter what else the company does for you.

Mapping McGregor's Theory X and Theory Y

Douglas McGregor's work is less well known to general managers, which is a shame as it focuses closely on management style (one of Herzberg's key dissatisfiers). McGregor brought out the effects of reactionary and over-zealous management practices and policies in his two models: Theory X and Theory Y.

Theory X assumes that, as a worker, you've an inbuilt dislike of working and shirk as much as you can get away with. Therefore, you need to be controlled to ensure that you put in the effort needed, and you need to be told exactly what to do and how to do it. This attitude can be damaging to your natural motivation, your job satisfaction, and eventually your self-belief and confidence. Studies suggest that if your boss treats you this way, you may begin to behave as if it were true. (If this situation is happening to you, use the feedback model in Chapter 15 to make this point to your supervisor or departmental representative.)

Theory Y takes the opposite view. It assumes that working is important to you, and as natural to you as the other parts of your life. If your work is satisfying, it becomes a source of drive and fulfilment, increasing your personal confidence. You become committed to it and you require little in the way of supervision.

You perform better and are more productive if you're allowed to manage your own workload, output, and so on, because you know so much better than anyone else how to get the best out of yourself. In these circumstances, your supervisor becomes a colleague you can consult when you need a second opinion and who can liaise with senior management to enable you to do the best job possible.

How do these two models compare with your own job situation? The chances are that your own supervision has elements of both Theory X and Theory Y. As ever, the onus is on you to take more control of an element of your life. When you have knowledge, you've the opportunity to put it confidently to use.

Taking action may require all the confidence you can muster, and in this case it repays you doubly by getting you what you want and by helping to build your confidence for the future.

The challenge you face is not so much individuals and their personal attitudes but organisation structures and the way jobs are organised. If you supervise a team, or even just work in a team, following Theory Y gives you a far better chance of getting the results you need. Educate your colleagues where you can and help to bring your teams into the 21st century.

Putting theory to the test

In this section, you see how to use the theoretical insights from the preceding sections to build your confidence as you engage with the world. And because most motivation theory is based on the workplace, you start there.

Whether you work for yourself or for someone else, you have to meet your motivational needs. Table 4-2 provides a self-test you can take in five minutes that measures your motivation response at work. If you work alone, modify the questions as necessary to suit your circumstances. Give yourself up to five points for each question – all five if you strongly agree, down to one if you strongly disagree.

Table 4-2	Job Motivation Response Self-Test				
Value Statement	**Strongly Agree (5 points)**	**Agree (4 points)**	**Neutral (3 points)**	**Disagree (2 point)**	**Strongly Disagree (1 point)**
I am entirely in control of my work environment. Provided I meet my objectives, I am free to decide how much I do and what work I do next.					
I have established a good working relationship with my boss. She gives me the room to do my job the way I want and I usually deliver what she needs.					
My benefits package and general working environment are okay. When something needs to be looked at, it is usually sorted out in a reasonable time.					
My work colleagues are generally supportive and don't get in my way. We are a good team and each of us serves the group objective pretty effectively. When issues arise, we are usually able to deal with them.					
I get a real buzz from the work I do. I feel closely identified with my output and put the best of myself into it. I wouldn't want it to be any other way.					

Value Statement	Strongly Agree (5 points)	Agree (4 points)	Neutral (3 points)	Disagree (2 point)	Strongly Disagree (1 point)
I feel that my employer values my work and is in touch with what is going on. They care about my career and look after things so that I don't have to worry about them.					
My work is highly visible. People know that it is mine, and I take great pride in it. It is not unusual for people to acknowledge the good job I am doing.					
I am allowed to take full responsibility for the quality of my work and for meeting my other objectives and deadlines. My boss knows that I know how to get the best out of myself and lets me get on with it.					
I feel that my work stretches me and allows me to grow. I have the level of challenge and variety that keeps me fully engaged without being overwhelmed.					
My work is an expression of who I truly am at a deeper level. Even if I weren't being paid, I'd still need to express myself through the work I do. If I were unable to work it would be like losing a limb.					

Use these guidelines to evaluate your score:

✔ **40–50:** Congratulations, you may have found your life's work. You're working in a job that gives you most of what you need not only for motivation but for your growth and fulfilment too.

✔ **30–40:** This score is good. You should be able to see the areas that are pulling you down and you can develop some goals for changing them. Use the SMART goal-setting technique in Chapter 3 to help create the changes you need.

✔ **10–30:** You may already know that this score isn't so good. You probably need to take more personal responsibility for your motivation at work, which can include changing your job or organization. Take a look at the techniques in Chapter 15 to help you take more control of your work.

Recognising the importance of achievement

Achieving results at work isn't just a matter of pleasing your boss and earning a bonus. It forms an important contribution to your personal sense of significance and wellbeing as you move confidently up the hierarchy of needs (see Figure 4-1) and a sense of achievement is top of the list of Herzberg's motivators (refer to Table 4-1).

As you progress at work, you need to think more about what constitutes achievement for *you.* Consider what you want out of your life and work, and then, without working any harder, you should be able to secure more of it both for yourself and your employer. Doing so increases your sense of fulfilment and satisfaction and provides you with more motivational energy for more confident achievement.

Your relationship to your work is an influential part of your relationship to the world and all it contains. To achieve the most confident and powerful version of yourself, you need to understand and manage your value and contribution through your work in the world.

Going for the next promotion

Like most people, when a promotion opportunity comes up, you may want to seize the chance to get it immediately (not least because if you don't get it someone else will). But think carefully about what the promotion may mean for you before you go for it.

A not-uncommon situation is for a successful and happy worker to win a promotion only to become a less successful and far less happy supervisor or manager. When this kind of promotion happens, the person can remain stuck in their new role where their poor performance rules out any further advancement and the organisational hierarchy prevents them from returning to where they were good and happy.

If you know anyone who has been caught in this way, you understand that this kind of problem is hardly a recipe for organisational achievement – much less for personal confidence and fulfilment. Armed with knowledge of this chapter, no reason remains why it should happen to you.

Before you accept any new role, ask yourself:

- ✔ How did things play out for the previous person who held this job? Perhaps they went on to even higher things, or perhaps they were stuck in the role for a long time and didn't appear too happy in it.

- ✔ What is likely to happen to you if you remain a while longer in your current role? Is there an even better promotion coming up soon? Would your refusal to take on the promotion offered send a bad or a good signal to your management?

- ✔ How can you use the current situation to create the job you want? Would it be possible to change the new job into something that suits you better, retaining, say, some of your current responsibility? Or perhaps it would be possible to split up the new role and take only some aspects of it into your current role?

- ✔ How can you use the change on offer to let your colleagues and superiors know that you're thinking deeply about the work you do and are not just in it for the next pay cheque? In the longer-term, this may be the most valuable aspect of the entire situation.

Now, when the opportunity for promotion comes up, you've a richer way of evaluating why you're interested in the new role, what it can bring to you other than money and what it can take away. And if you decide to go for it, you bring so much more to the table; acting confidently and making a good impression on your colleagues and leaving you with a big win whether or not you get the role.

Chapter 5

Sticking to Your Principles

● ●

In This Chapter

▶ Identifying your values

▶ Creating the life you've always wanted

▶ Leading an authentic life

● ●

*I*f you knew what was most important to you in life and spent 70 or 80 years becoming really good at it, would the quality of your life be improved, do you think? Would this knowledge enable you to be a lot clearer about your priorities? Would you be more confident in cutting down on things that don't contribute to your fulfilment, and cutting out altogether those things that actually take you away from what you want? You bet it would!

Defining what you truly want and how you want to live, and then sticking to your principles, is your most powerful means of generating the confidence to achieve a life you love. In this chapter, you discover the things your life is really about and how to bring them to fruition.

Understanding Your Values

What do you value most in life – what is most important to you? These questions are probably the most important ones a human being can face and yet many people don't know the answers. If you want to bring your most confident version of yourself into the world and live a life truly worthy of you, it's important that you can answer them. You can then use your answers to guide you through life. This chapter is designed to help you discover your answers and live accordingly.

Discovering your values

It's an odd thing, but when you really get down to it, if you're like most people, you may have only a broad idea of how you want your life to be. You certainly want to be happy and may feel that to be confident about being happy you need certain other things: such as good health, a good job, a suitable partner, perhaps a loving family, maybe a nice home and a decent car (maybe even a *very* nice car). On top of these things, you've certain values that you feel need to be fulfilled: values such as honesty, integrity, respect, and so on. Beyond these values, many people are unsure.

If you're in this position, take heart. The work you do in this chapter helps to clarify your values, leaving you crystal clear and confident about what makes you happy, and making it far more likely that you can achieve what you want.

Think about this deceptively simple question: what do you value most in life? What comes immediately to mind? Is it highly personal things – your health, your loved ones? Does it involve your work or sense of vocation – your art, your work at the hospital? Is your immediate thought of big, global issues – ecology, poverty, or world peace?

In discovering your most important values – those things that you believe will lead you to the feelings you most want in your life – go for those things that really engage you emotionally and leave out the things that you feel you *ought* to care most about; there should be no 'oughts' in this exercise (apart from that one!). With that proviso, you're ready to begin:

1. **Write down your answer to the question: What is most important to me in my life? Write down the single most important thing.**

2. **Now answer the similar question: What else is most important to me in my life? Write down the next most important thing.**

3. **And finally, answer for the third time: What else is most important to me in my life? Write down the third most important thing.**

You can stop now, as you've three answers to work with, which is plenty for your first time; but you would only have to keep going to get more.

The answers you write down we call your *means values* because these values are the means by which you're pursuing what you want in your life (don't worry if this sentence doesn't make much sense to you yet).

No such thing exists as a right or wrong answer here. What you're finding out is what you want in life and ultimately how you can confidently get more of it into your daily living. By doing the work in this chapter, you become able to include in your life the things that are most important to you. If you do so, you will care more about what you're doing and you'll be more powerful and confident.

Uncovering your ends values

If your means values are your means to an end, then what is this end they're supposed to help you achieve? The answer to this question is key, so are you ready for it? The answer is *feelings*! How you feel, at any point in your day, largely drives how you behave and how you *are* in the world. How you feel colours everything you do, and you discovered at an early age to manage the way you feel by trying to have more of some things and less of others.

Your *means values* are your grown-up version of your need to satisfy your inner child's wanting to feel a certain way. They may not be the only ways you can get these feelings, and they may not be the best ways, but you have them linked together in your mind and are pursuing your desired feelings by these means.

Wow! So all those difficult things you've been pursuing in life are just to help you to feel a certain way? Yes, and it would be helpful right now to work out exactly what feelings you want to feel. These feelings are your *ends values*.

To elicit your ends values from your means values, follow these steps:

1. **Write down the first means value that you uncovered when you asked yourself: 'What is most important to me in my life?'**

   As an example, Dave is a married man whose first means value is his family.

2. **Now ask yourself the supplementary question: 'If I have this, what does it give me?'**

   Dave's answer to this question is 'a reason to get up in the morning to provide for them'.

3. **And now ask yourself the further supplementary question of the answer you just came up with: 'And what will *that* give me?'**

   Applying the question elicits from Dave: 'a reason for being active and powerful in the world'.

4. **Repeat Steps 2 and 3 until you arrive at a *basic emotion or feeling* (such as safety, love, connection, and so on).**

   In Dave's case, asking the question again gives: 'deliver my maximum value to the world', and once again gives: 'I'll be able to look at myself in the mirror', which finally comes down to 'self-respect'.

   Dave can stop at this point, because self-respect is a basic feeling that he gets from looking after his wife and children. Providing for his family may also contribute to other feelings, but we'll stick with self-respect for now because this answer is what came up.

5. **Repeat the process with the other answers you gave to the question: 'What is most important to me in my life?'**

   By repeating the questioning process on all your means values, you eventually arrive at a few basic feelings, usually not more than half a dozen. These feelings are your *ends values,* the basic feelings you want to experience regularly in your life.

6. **Write down all the basic feelings, or ends values, that you come up with.**

   Dave came up with the ends values of self-respect, connection, health and vitality, playfulness, and wisdom.

Congratulations! When you've completed this exercise, pause a moment to reflect on what you've just achieved. In terms of your personal development, you're now ahead of 90 per cent of the people on the planet. *You know what you've been trying to achieve in your life so far and why.* These feelings on your list are your ultimate values and everything else is just your means of achieving them. You work with your list throughout this chapter.

As soon as you have your lists of feelings, or ends values, you're in a position to work with them in ways that can assist you to get them into your life more easily, frequently and confidently. When you can do that, your values are satisfied and you're free to get on with your life in a whole new and liberated way. Your confidence is unbounded.

Resolving values conflicts

You may find that two or more of your means values are pulling you in different directions. For example, many people have both family and job on their list of what's most important to them. Both enable you to experience the feelings of connection, achievement, success, and so on that you want in your life.

However, trying to honour both simultaneously can spread you thin and sometimes leave you feeling stressed, worrying that you're not doing well with your values in either area. At its worst, you may feel when you're working that you should be spending more with your family, and when you're with the family you feel you should be working. From here you can become prey to feelings you definitely do *not* want in your life such as guilt, frustration, and dissatisfaction.

If this sort of values conflict strikes a chord with you, take heart. Resolving such conflicts can add a lot to the quality of your life.

With a little work and application, you can turn such a confidence-sapping 'no win' into a confidence-boosting 'no lose'. Before you can do so, though, you need to know about values hierarchies and rules.

Rating your values

In Chapter 4, we talk about Maslow's Hierarchy of Needs and how to use it. Maslow's Hierarchy of Needs is a generalised model of values that illustrates the influences on everyone. But armed with the knowledge in this chapter, you can go a step further. Here you discover your own, totally personal hierarchy of values. Although largely unconscious, your personal hierarchy has become tailored to the specifics of your life, and working with it is important for ensuring that it serves you.

All your values are important, but you will always choose to secure one or two of them first in order to be able to enjoy the others.

Take a little time now to rank the ends values you discovered in the preceding 'Uncovering your ends values' section into a hierarchy, putting the most important one at the top and so on down to the last.

When you've completed this list, go on to the next section, which shows you how to make it really easy to have your values met, and much more difficult to feel that they've been violated.

Making your own rules

How is it that two people, on the same fairground ride, may have such a totally different experience of the ride? One may feel terrified and hate every second of it, while the other gets a 'rush' and a sense of exhilaration. What's happening here comes down to a particular set of beliefs they each carry around with them and use to determine whether or not their values are being met. These special beliefs – which you have, as well – are your rules about your values.

What's actually happening physically on the fairground ride is virtually the same for each person. But what each person experiences and therefore feels can be completely differ-ent. Each of them is unconsciously applying a specific set of beliefs about their physical experience in the form of rules. The rule for one person may be something like 'I am putting myself in danger irresponsibly and pointlessly' and the rule for the other is 'I love the thrill of speed, it makes me feel so alive'.

All beliefs help you to make decisions quickly based on previous experience, but when they take the form of unconscious rules they may be working against you and causing you feelings that you don't want.

You don't have to worry about where your rules came from – whether you've an easy guess about the source or not. Because your rules are merely beliefs, that is, merely a sense of certainty, you can change them easily by applying a little common sense.

If you're in a similar situation, ask yourself: 'how likely is it that this fairground ride is going to crash in a serious accident, involving me as a victim, at this precise moment?' The real odds don't matter; the grounds for worry are so tiny. Is it a reasonable belief then, that you will be seriously injured on this ride on this occasion? No, it isn't. This belief doesn't stand up. Now, apply a similar logic to find any benefit that may ensue from your taking the ride and keep looking until you find some.

Beliefs like this one, if they do not immediately respond to the logic treatment, may prove to be *phobias*. They can also be removed relatively easily but you may need the assistance of a therapist as described in Chapter 9.

The exciting part is: What can you now consciously *choose* to believe about this situation instead of the false belief? Well, it would be frightening and exciting perhaps (call this *exhilaration*), and you would feel afterwards the glow of having achieved something that you haven't achieved before (call this *personal growth*). You can also share the experience of the ride with your friends now instead of waiting at the bottom with all the coats and bags (call this *connection*).

Your new rule may be that *you feel a sense of exhilaration, growth, and connection each time you stretch yourself to do something new with your friends.* How much better would this attitude work in bringing the values you want into your life? How much more confidently would you approach new experiences?

To change any of your rules, you simply have to choose an alternative that works better for you – one that brings you pleasure rather than the pain of the old rule. You may reasonably question whether this line of reasoning is a bit fake and, in a way, you're right. But don't dignify your current rules as any more 'real'. They're no more real than the new set that you now choose, and if you choose your new rules well, they will be a lot more effective in allowing you to feel confident about any way you want to feel.

For example, Raj's top value is to feel healthy and vital, but his old rules for experiencing this value were: I must have a good workout at the gym three times a week, and run five miles three times a week, and be within 3 pounds of my ideal weight, and be eating only nourishing, water-rich foods, and have no pain anywhere in my body.

Unfortunately, Raj wasn't able easily to satisfy all these rules at the same time so he didn't feel healthy and vital often. When he changed his rules, the problem was magically fixed. He expressed his new rules for feeling healthy and vital in the form of affirmations, which he can repeat as often as he needs to keep them firmly in his mind:

- ✔ I am aware of how healthy and vital I feel whenever I exercise to a warm glow.

- ✔ I am aware of how healthy and vital I feel whenever I go to bed without feeling exhausted.

- ✔ I am aware of how healthy and vital I feel whenever I avoid poor food or drink choices.

- ✔ I am aware of how healthy and vital I feel whenever I walk rather than ride.

- ✔ I am aware of how healthy and vital I feel whenever I meditate.

Ask yourself what has to happen in order for you to feel that sense of connection you want so badly. How about simply stopping for a moment in your busy day and picturing your partner, or children, or parents, whatever it is for you. That can be enough to flood you with feelings of connectedness. Don't limit yourself to one thing, though; add in some more.

Create half a dozen new rules that allow you to experience each of the values in your hierarchy. Make your own list of affirmations for each end's value.

Using your affirmations can ensure that you feel the way you want to feel most of the time, and it eliminates the values conflicts that come from the limitation of having many hard-to-satisfy rules about fulfilling your values.

By giving yourself a variety of ways to feel good, you set yourself up for success and self-confidence because fulfilling your alternative rules or affirmations as you go through your day is easier.

Living Your Values Every Day

When you're conscious of your values, and you've a consistent set of achievable rules for experiencing their presence in your life, you've all you need to live life as a series of near-perfect days. In the following sections, you discover how to make this ideal a reality.

Doing these few things, which take just a few minutes each day, can transform your daily experience of living more surely than anything else you can do. You will be more confident and more in control of your achievements and experience of life. You'll be able to manage your values and feelings in a much more proactive way, creating new and more powerful meaning every day.

Try following the advice in the next three sections for a week and you'll be amazed by the transformation.

Focusing on what's important

Every night before you turn out the light, write down the half-dozen most important things you want to do tomorrow. The tasks can be anything at all, so long as they're the important things. While you sleep, your unconscious mind works out for you how you can achieve your aims most easily.

In the morning, before you get out of bed, take your list and decide how to fit the tasks and activities you've chosen into your day. If it looks like a tight fit, leave out the least important, and the next least until it looks sensible to you.

You now have a day's schedule that should ensure that both your time and your energy are focused on *the most important* activities of the day.

Sprinkling your values through your day

But this schedule is not yet enough to create a day when you live and fully experience the feelings you most want in life. To help ensure that you get these feelings into your day, simply bring your ends values to mind one by one and use your value affirmations to see where in your schedule you've the greatest likelihood of feeling that value. The opportunity may be easily present in several places: just bring each occasion to mind and envision your day with all such opportunities taken.

Now you're much more likely to *live* your perfect day, focused on the important activities and enriched by your most valued feelings. You've become present to the way the day *can* be and are much more likely to *experience it* that way.

Reviewing your day

At the end of your day, mentally review what happened and how you experienced it. Perhaps the day worked out pretty much as you planned it, but you didn't get everything done that you thought you would. You can discover new realities from this review; maybe you habitually give yourself too much to do. Instead of beating yourself up for not completing your to-do list, make a note to limit what you take on until you get the balance right.

Perhaps your day didn't work out the way you intended at all. Maybe an unexpected crisis arose at work or something else just came up. That's okay. Reflect on whether you managed to live your values anyway. Did you have that sense of connection, or feel the love when you thought of the family and took a moment to feel how lucky you are to have them?

Whatever happened is fine; don't judge it, just look at what actually happened today and write down the most important things you want to get done tomorrow. Then go to sleep.

Living Authentically

By now you should be able to see that out in the world is where things are happening; inside you, an entirely personal set of experiences and feelings is being generated in response to what is occurring; and all these occurrences add to the totality of your life to date. In a very real way, you inhabit the inside world of feelings and meaning much more than the external world of current events. This insight is massive and transformational.

Because meaning is largely a matter of your interpretation and choice, personal transformation is not only possible but can happen in this instant. For it to happen to you, you need to free yourself to interpret events and create the meaning that works for you, without the need to consult or ask permission of anyone else. How you're experiencing life is inside you, and you've a lot more leeway and room for individuality than you may have realised.

To aid your growth and to help you fine-tune your sense of who you are and what you can be and do in the world, an important step is to trust your developing self-awareness in the face of resistance from those who think that they know you best, and even those who love you best. Be authentic, be true to yourself, and you really begin to make progress. This authenticity is another key to your power and confidence in the world.

There may be a time when you can lead those who most care about you through a similar journey of their own. For now, you need to be fully committed to your own development and you need to trust in your ability to see it through. All you need to do to become the fully authentic version of yourself is to stop pretending:

- Stop pretending to be what you're not; stop pretending not to be what you really are.

- Stop pretending to care about things you don't care about; stop pretending not to care about the things you do.

- Stop pretending to believe in things that you don't; stop pretending not to believe in the things you really do.

Now ask yourself: What do I really stand for? What do I really care about? What do I truly believe in? If your answers to these questions begin to differ from those you worked with earlier in this chapter, you can go back and do the real work more confidently with your new, authentic answers. The difference will be transformational.

Developing your identity

Finding out how to be true to yourself is critical, and letting this developing version of yourself become known in the world is also important. You need to let your friends and colleagues know that you've begun to think about things in new ways and that you're determined to take control of your life. This step is an important one, but it can be difficult as your changing can easily unsettle or even threaten those around you.

The gay movement has a name for the psychological and social repositioning that accompanies a homosexual man or woman reclaiming their authentic identity: They call it *coming out*. Although your coming out as your authentic self is unlikely to entail the same social risks and consequences, the stages you have to pass through are similar.

The *Cass Model* describes six stages of developing identity; it has been adapted here to suit our present purpose.

Stage 1: Confusion

In this first stage, the identity you've always taken for granted is called into question. You may be confused as you begin to feel that your previous roles as reliable friend, helpful sister, caring mother, conscientious worker, and so on miss the essence of who you truly are. 'But who would I still be if I were none of these things?' becomes a legitimate enquiry in search of your more authentic self.

Stage 2: Comparison

In this stage, you may be thinking that you're in some respects more self-aware or otherwise different from your family, friends, and most other people in your social network. This thought can set off a fear of rejection and you may adopt strategies to minimise the risks (such as not telling anyone about your growing dissatisfaction with the status quo).

You may begin reading self-help books surreptitiously or see a coach or counsellor confidentially. You may conclude that you only have issues at work, and in all other respects you're just as you always were.

The best advice for you is to go easy on yourself. You cannot rush personal change and holding it back is just as difficult. Let it take its course, reading any books and listening to any recordings that help you. You may not feel ready yet to take on the world and you don't have to.

Stage 3: Tolerance

By this stage, you may no longer be satisfied with your previous experience of life (regardless of how successful you are in the eyes of the world). Although you may still be unclear about your life's meaning and destiny, and therefore still lack the confidence to make a change, you're likely to be getting used to the idea of being on some kind of development journey.

You may have sought out a few like-minded souls, though the gulf between your growing sense of self and others all around you is growing even greater. This stage can be an especially trying one if you've a strong need for peer approval and acceptance.

Stage 4: Acceptance

Publicly you may still be pretending to be as you always were, but inside you have accepted the difference and are feeling changed irrevocably. You're addressing the issues of 'Who am I really?' and 'How do I truly fit in?'

Stages 5 and 6: Pride and Synthesis

In these closely allied stages, you move from your growing 'them' and 'me' mentality into a realisation and acceptance that your experience of the world has fundamentally shifted rather than the world itself.

You remain a part of it all, just as you always have, with a heightened awareness of your authentic self-identity and increased ability to live your values and 'walk your talk'. Your authentic self is stronger and more confident and you feel less threatened by what the world may throw at you.

This last phase is your heroic identity, your fully authentic self delivered daily into the world through the medium of your chosen mission and values: your hero's journey. You may feel unstoppable. Your experience of living your values is powerful and complete.

Facing up to your demons

Your journey to your truly authentic self is a lifelong project. And just like the heroes of Greek and Roman mythology (and the superheroes of comic books and Hollywood) you will choose to face your demons.

A demon in our modern world is anything that you fear, and fail to face. Demons are precisely the things that have been holding you back, and the confidence to take action is what you need to overcome them. This book is full of advice you can use to build your confidence so use it and get out there to face your personal demons and live your life on a more heroic scale.

For the most part, you can face your tests with confidence and a keen sense of purposeful engagement. Some challenges, though, are frightening and lonely. During these trials, keep in mind that life was going to give you these tests anyway, and at least now you're getting them on your own terms and in a worthy cause.

In these dark moments, reflect on your progress so far and give yourself a pat on the back for achieving so much. If you're tired, take rest; if you're confused, take advice. You always have the choice of moving confidently forward into growth or backward into fear. When you're ready, choose growth.

World champion track athlete Steve Cram said something that may help you get your head around all this. At the time he was the 1,500 metres world champion and world record holder. Injured, and temporarily laid up, he was doing a TV promotion at a charity event. The amateur runners had given their all and some of them were in terrible shape, collapsing on the line, being ill, and so on. On live TV a commentator asked Steve whether he had ever felt so totally used up in this way. Steve's response: 'It is exactly the same for me every time I run. I feel the same pain as these guys, I just run a lot quicker.'

You've choices in life and you can expect highs and lows whatever path you choose. Like Steve Cram, you can raise your standards to those of the world's best and experience them from there. Why should you accept anything less than the world champion version of yourself? You don't have to, so don't.

Chapter 6

Making Friends with Your Emotions

*T*hink back over the last week and you're likely to recall running through a wide range of emotions. Happiness, love, joy, fear, sadness, anger, and guilt are all natural human responses in everyday life.

Emotions are important in building your confidence because they drive your behaviour and how you feel about yourself. Emotions also have an enormous impact on your body and your health (you can read more about the mind–body connection in Chapter 10.)

This chapter helps you get in tune with how you experience the reality of life through how you feel – good and bad, up and down.

Getting a Grip on Your Emotions

When you make friends with your emotions, you listen to them and get to know them better. In this way, you gain vital information about what is happening to you and take responsibility for your response. By raising your self-awareness, you're in a stronger position to motivate yourself and confidently take the action you want, rather than reacting to other people and circumstances.

You may be asking yourself why you'd ever want to get angry or fearful – wouldn't it be good to drop these 'friends' out of your repertoire? Definitely not! Even your most negative emotions have their place in looking after you. They mean that you're alive and real. Your job is to notice your emotional reactions and focus the energy from them appropriately. In the following sections, we help you do just that.

Accessing your emotional intelligence

Popularised by author Daniel Goleman, the concept of *emotional intelligence (EQ)* relates to being able to rein in your emotional impulses, to read another's innermost feelings, and to handle relationships smoothly. The precepts of EQ are increasingly valued in business and other walks of life, such as education, as organisations realise their tangible impact on profitability.

Emotional intelligence relates to a range of competencies around two aspects:

- ✔ **Personal competence:** How you handle yourself, your awareness of your feelings, and your understanding of your capabilities.

- ✔ **Social competence:** How you handle relationships with other people; in particular, how you manage your unhelpful reactions, how you exhibit empathy, and how much flexibility you demonstrate in dealing with difficult situations.

Whether you're a student or the chairman of a company, your ability to manage your emotions and bring out the best in others can make the difference between success and failure. Lose your temper and you lose an important customer or damage an important relationship – and the rest, as they say, is history.

The good news is that you can improve your emotional intelligence over time. Your EQ is not a given that you're born with and are stuck with. A number of formal assessment tools on the market help you understand the fine dimensions of emotional intelligence and how you score.

To get the real benefit of a formal tool, feedback from other people is useful, as is taking a self-assessment test. Take this test with the support of a development partner, coach or mentor because the information you receive may be challenging to handle on your own.

Pitting rational thought against emotion

Each time you think about an event in the past, you recall it slightly differently. Usually, over time, the intensity of the emotion becomes lessened. However, some memories may continue to really annoy or upset you, especially if the memory is of something that was unjust or unfair or an event you feel embarrassed about. Part of you wants to be logical and rational about it, yet part of you still doesn't want to let go of it. Every time you think about it, the old tug of emotion gets to you. One way to move on is to separate your memory of an event from the emotion involved.

 If a negative memory still conjures up strong emotion, you can try to distance yourself from the memory. Picture the event as something that happened a long time ago. See it as a faded black-and-white photograph with no colour, no life and no emotional pull at all.

 Use the Event, Memory, Emotion, Knowledge, and Action steps outlined here to overcome the negative effects of your memories:

1. **Recall the Event:** What was the event that happened to you?

   As an example, we use the case of Heather, who suffered from intense nerves and failed her driving test six times. The Event for her was her failed driving test.

2. **Recover the Memory:** What is your memory of that event?

   Heather's Memory is meeting the driving instructor and getting into the car.

3. **Evaluate your Emotion:** What emotion do you experience when you access that memory? On a scale of 1 (weak) to 10 (strong) how strong is your emotion?

   Heather's Emotion is a feeling of fear and worry in her stomach, which rates an 8 out 10.

4. **Uncover the underlying Knowledge:** What knowledge can you take from the memory that can help you in the future?

   Heather's Knowledge is managing her nerves when driving with a stranger in the passenger seat.

5. **Decide on an Action:** What action can you take as a result?

   Heather's Action is to book her next three driving lessons with three different instructors.

By going through these steps, you can extract the value of the memory to boost your confidence and take the lesson forward while letting go of the downside of all the negative emotion.

Connecting creativity and confidence

The last 30 years have seen a tremendous amount of research into how the brain operates, and the field of neuroscience continues to broaden our understanding of the human experience.

However, taking a straightforward, practical concept of division of labour in the brain suggests that the two hemispheres of the brain process information in different ways. The left hemisphere is responsible for verbal, analytical, and logical processing, while the right side processes information in a more global, intuitive, and creative way – and it needs unpressured time and space to do that. (In left-handed people, this division of labour works the other way around.)

Creativity is about using imagination to make something new that didn't exist before – whether this something is an idea, or something more tangible like a piece of art or literature. It usually involves seeing the connection between seemingly unrelated things. Most successful individuals deliberately allow time and space for their creative imagination to get to work – which is right-brained activity. Unfortunately, with business pressures growing, many companies overlook the need to allow people time to brainstorm and engage all aspects of their creativity.

Building your own confidence involves finding new ideas, approaches, and solutions. To do so, you must use both parts of your brain and allow the creativity to flood in rather than shutting part of it down.

Take regular time out on your own to think and re-charge your batteries.

Finding courage to voice your emotions

Trusting yourself to express emotion takes courage. It may be particularly hard if you're used to operating in a cool, factual, and rational way. Yet it is through your emotions that you can connect with yourself and with other people in a deeper, more confident way.

Clearly it isn't appropriate to tell everyone at work your inner-most emotions or pent-up feelings, but you probably have room to express yourself more fully than you are currently. Consider whether you've one area of your life in which you're holding back your emotional reactions and feelings. Do you ever feel there's something important to say but you never quite manage to say it? Try to determine the long-term benefit if you voice what you really think and feel.

Any relationship based on an open and honest expression of feelings has a strong chance of staying fresh and engaging – it continues to grow rather than stagnate.

Sharing the love at work

Beppe is the managing director of a building company. Through attending a personal development course, he realised just how hard he found expressing his emotions, and he discovered how to tell his family how much he loved them. But at work, where he was also used to operating in a macho style, he continued managing through the financial figures and productivity measures.

One day when business was tough, he decided to be courageous and express his feelings to his fellow directors. He began the monthly board meeting by going to each member of the team around the table and saying how much he appreciated them and what he really valued in them. The team was surprised and also delighted to see this more human side of the MD.

As a result, the meeting got straight to the heart of difficult issues and made important decisions that people had been holding back on.

Tracking Your Moods

During the course of a day, you experience a number of *moods* – temporary states of mind or temper. Think of your moods as a temperature gauge, registering hot and cold at different times according to the weather.

Whatever mood you're in affects your behaviour and this behaviour in turn has an impact on the results you get. When you feel energetic and enthusiastic, you naturally take on more and confidently get more done. So a real benefit can come from paying attention to how you feel. Your mood shows through your expressions and gestures as much as by what you say or don't say, and thus has a knock-on effect on others around you.

If you're aware that you're not in your best frame of mind, then you know instinctively that you're not in the best place from which to make important decisions. If your mood isn't helpful, the quickest thing you can do is change it by changing your physical state. Have a nap or go for a run or a swim; if all else fails, have a cup of coffee.

Staying in touch with your mood patterns

As you refine your awareness of your mood and that of other people, you heighten your observation of what triggers a change in mood for you – whether for good or bad.

As you become more aware of your moods, think about the colours and hues of your underlying emotions and feelings, the fine difference in temperature that you detect in yourself and those around you.

Take a typical day in your schedule, once a week, and make a note of your mood at key points in the day – early in the morning, at midday, mid-afternoon, early evening, and finally as you go to bed.

Start to pay attention to how you're feeling and the nuances of how you describe those feelings. On the down side, you may say that you're sad, grumpy, sullen, nervy, melancholy, or cross. And when things are on the up you may be happy, content, peaceful, excited, or joyful. You'll soon see how some feelings are more conducive to confident action. Start to build your own repertoire of language to describe the subtle changes in your mood, and pay attention to what happens to trigger the change. You may then decide you want to make some changes in your day to prevent yourself dropping into a weakened state.

Becoming more aware of your natural state

When Kate is walking along, she often finds herself involuntarily humming a familiar piece of classical music – *Vltava,* by the Bohemian composer Smetana. Her humming transports her to a happy, sociable time when she heard it played in a concert. She takes her humming to mean that all is well with the world, she's in a good state, and that her life is flowing steadily.

Facing up to overwhelm

Jhoti is a businessman who has built up a profitable food manufacturing empire. As a hard-working entrepreneur, he lived his life in a constant state of stress and being overwhelmed. He rushed from meeting to meeting, never taking time out to think or plan but responding to an increasing number of crises. He became aware of the effect of his mental anxiety on his body and the stress on his heart and blood pressure. He realised that it affected his ability to make decisions clearly and act confidently. He chose to employ a coach to work with him on re-assessing his personal and business goals.

Your *state* is more than just a mood – but a way of being, as opposed to a way of doing. To find your natural state, your baseline state on a day-to-day basis, you need to determine your normal way of being. For example, are you naturally laid back about life most of the time, or do you go through life with a purposeful energy racing inside you? Do you have a strong sense of nervous excitement, anxiety, or guilt, or do you live in limbo waiting and anticipating what will happen next?

Your baseline state is how you're used to being as you go about your life. This state has become a habit. You may be happy with it or want to change it. By noticing what your baseline state is like, you're in a good position to adapt it where and when you want to.

At the start of each day, set your intent for the state you want to be in for the day. Check in with yourself at intervals in the day to see how you're doing.

Life has a natural rhythm of ups and downs. However, if you regularly experience negative feelings of being overwhelmed or anxious – more than, say, 20 per cent of the time – then make an appointment to see your doctor or medical practitioner.

You can decide to be confident (that is, to take powerful, appropriate action) in any state or mood; but it takes less energy to make this decision from some states than others.

Trusting Your Intuition

You have it, but how well do you use it? Intuition is your gut feeling, the magical sense inside that can guide you if you listen to it. Intuition often comes in a flash of insight, an 'aha!' moment. *Intuition* can be defined as 'the direct knowing of something without the conscious use of reasoning'. Intuition is what you have when you pay real attention to your kind and helpful unconscious mind. When you get in touch with your intuition, you connect with what you really want in your life – and follow that true sense of direction that confident people have.

Tuning in to the gifts of intuition

Listening to your intuition gives you valuable information about what is really going on for you at a deeper level. When you listen to your inner self, you become connected to the energy within your body – physically, emotionally, and spiritually. Your intuition may or may not give you the 'right' answer, but working with it rather than against it can be incredibly valuable.

Your intuition can help you to:

✔ Find new ways around problems.

✔ Make sense of a situation.

✔ Improve your decision-making abilities.

✔ Notice things that need your attention.

✔ Achieve your goals.

How can you know when your intuition is kicking in? When you find yourself thinking: *This is strange,* or *how bizarre,* or *what a coincidence.* You may get an insight that you're letting go of the rational and logical thoughts and just going with what feels right. To find out more about how to access your intuition, check out the Art of Intuition's website at www. artofintuition.co.uk. They offer UK workshops and information. You can also check out Laura Day's www. practicalintuition.com US site.

Faking it

Traditionally, women have been the ones who've had the edge on the 'sixth sense'. Maybe now the tables are turning. It would seem that men are getting in touch with their intuitive side, according to a study carried out at Edinburgh Science Festival by the University of Hertfordshire. Researchers asked 15,000 people to look at images of smiling faces and pick out the 'real' grins. Men spotted 76 per cent of the women's fake smiles, while women only identified 67 per cent of men's fake smiles.

Listening to your inner self

Einstein said that problems can't be solved at the same level at which they're created. Great scientists as well as great artists, musicians, and leaders in every field act on their hunches to achieve breakthroughs in their thinking.

You can release your own intuition by using your imagination to think about problems in a completely different way. To do so, use this exercise when you're grappling with a challenge:

1. **State your issue to yourself.**

2. **Let go of the facts and quiet your rational mind.**

3. **Sit in silence without interruption for 15 minutes.**

4. **Open yourself to the intuitive insights that come to you.**

   You may become aware of visual images, sensations in your body, or a connection with a particular person or place.

5. **Allow your analytical mind to wake up and get to work on the intuitive thoughts.**

The saying goes: 'People buy on emotion and justify on facts.' Whether you're selling yourself at an interview, promoting an idea, or selling a product to a client, take notice of the emotional undercurrents at play as well as the factual evidence. You can be sure that these play a part.

Harnessing Your Darker Emotions

Dark emotions are part of life and part of who you are, just as night follows day. They can create great energy for confident action, although you should take care that negative emotions do not flow into action unchecked. To have the power confidence brings is one thing, but to use that power for good is another. Negative emotions can cloud your judgement.

Some emotions stimulate your energy while others depress it. Fear and anger, for example, stimulate you to action. Meanwhile, sadness and guilt act as depressants, causing you to hold back and lie low. Unless they're regularly diffused, emotions can build over time to a point where they erupt uncontrollably.

Picture the emotional events in your life like a bracelet of beads on a string. Imagine experiencing anger over the years and not being able to express your feelings: At age 5, your favourite toy is given away without your permission; at age 11, you get bullied in the school playground; at age 15, the first person you have a crush on dumps you for someone else; at age 18, you lose out on a competition prize because someone else cheated; at age 25, you get gazumped on a house purchase. Finally, at age 30, you fail to make your putt on the final hole, lose the golf tournament, and your anger blows up uncontrollably.

Such seemingly unprovoked or over-the-top reactions often result when you subconsciously join up a number of 'angry' moments over your life into one big grievance. The explosion is way larger than the small, last-straw event that triggered it.

Unless you discover how to break this pattern, you're in danger of falling out with people unnecessarily – not an emotionally intelligent place to be. But also remember that all your emotions are valuable – they provide feedback about what is happening to you.

In the following sections, we look at some examples of finding the daylight in the darker moments.

Turning your anger into energy

By turning your anger into energy in a productive way, you stand more chance of getting the results you want. And the more you achieve this result, the more confidence you have in your ability to harness your darker emotions. For example, to handle a situation in which you're angry with someone, you need to express your feelings specifically and effectively. Resist the temptation to bring up every other little thing they've done to make you angry in the past. Things you've never mentioned before.

Knowing the difference between making a complaint and conducting a personal character assassination helps: a *complaint* is a remark about an action someone has taken that hasn't met with your expectation; a *personal criticism* is made about the person who failed to act appropriately. Make sure that you separate the 'deed' from the 'doer'.

A personal criticism leaves the other person feeling emotionally charged and defensive, which usually puts them onto the attack, and you both end up in a vicious downward spiral. Saying to your teenage child 'You're thoughtless, self-centred, and lazy' is a personal attack that encourages the anger to build and makes it even less likely that they're going to be ready on time or tidy up their bedroom.

Better instead to go for the complaint approach, being specific about what someone has done and how you feel as a result. A more productive complaint is: 'You left all the washing up for me to do, and I feel fed up in the kitchen doing it on my day off.' Follow that with a request for action: 'Please will you do your washing up after you've finished lunch?' You express your anger and make a reasonable request for change. A complaint allows for the energy to shift towards a resolution rather than wasting it in a red-faced exchange of temper.

When making a complaint, follow these steps:

1. **State the facts.**

2. **State your feelings.**

3. **Request a simple action.**

Forgiveness in the animal kingdom

Offering forgiveness to those who do you wrong is a sign of compassion. Studies among animals demonstrate amazing capability to sort out arguments and move on. Animals can't afford to hold a grudge in situations where they depend on each other for food or for competing against other groups. Yet humans seem to find conflict resolution much harder.

A *New Scientist* report ('Kiss and make up', 7 May 2005) looks at disputes between various animals from hyenas to dolphins. Chimps get top marks for instigating reconciliation. In one field study, researchers observe a male chimp leader slapping a female as he passes her. Within 15 minutes, she has licked her wounds and is the first to make amends by going to her attacker and offering the back of her hand for a kiss. Quickly, the group is happily reunited, cuddling, and sharing food once more.

Letting go of unhelpful emotions

Emotions such as jealousy and bitterness turn in on themselves, wrecking your self-belief and ability to take confident action. They eat away at you, taking up inordinate amounts of time and energy, and they prevent you from moving forward.

These feelings dissipate over time, but you can speed up their departure by using the Event, Memory, Emotion, Knowledge exercise in the 'Pitting rational thought against emotion' section earlier in this chapter.

If you still find yourself going over and over old wounds or grievances, seek professional therapeutic help to get closure on them. A Time Line Therapist can work with you to clean up on the negative emotions holding you back from enjoying life to the full.

Allowing yourself to forgive and move on

The art of developing mature relationships lies in the skills of managing yourself and empathising with other people. Daniel Goleman, in his work *Emotional Intelligence,* suggests that the roots of morality are to be found in empathy.

To have a mature relationship with someone takes *empathy* – the ability to enter into and share another person's emotions. When you face a difficult situation with someone, try to step into their shoes and understand what life looks like from their perspective, how they may be thinking or feeling about the situation.

Empathy is an attribute notably lacking in criminals. Bear this fact in mind if you're attacked or victimised, and always make your safety your prime concern.

Holding onto grievances from the past can deplete your energy. The memory of it can get in the way of you moving on with your life.

Give a message of forgiveness to someone you feel has upset or wronged you in the past by writing a letter to that person. Write down the facts around the incident that happened and how you felt about it at the time. Tell them that you forgive them for their part in the experience. You don't need to post the letter. You can now tear it up and see it disappear into the rubbish knowing that you've let go of whatever it was that upset you.

Reprogramming phobias

Some emotional responses are particularly tricky to change. A *phobia*, which is a severe, usually irrational response of fear, can be tenacious and difficult to dislodge. Phobias don't appear to be logical, and you may have no conscious idea of how the fear developed. Whether the phobia is of flying, escalators, motorway bridges, spiders, frogs, or anything else, the impact on your life can be hugely restrictive.

As coaches trained in Neuro-linguistic Programming, we work with clients using the *NLP fast phobia cure,* a technique that enables you to detach the emotional content from the memory of your experience.

The cure is explained fully in *Neuro-linguistic Programming For Dummies* (Wiley), of which Kate is co-author with Romilla Ready. Essentially the treatment is about separating yourself from the memory of a phobic response. The technique enables many people who've suffered phobias for years to have a cure within 20 minutes. The relief and pleasure of freedom from a phobia are extraordinarily powerful. Most importantly, people who overcome phobias regain control of their emotional responses.

Chapter 7

Unleashing Your Passion

*A*n important part of living your values (a topic we cover in Chapter 5) has to do with the intensity with which you live. If values are colours on your artist's palette, you'll want all your favourite colours, of course. But to paint a full and rich picture of your life, you surely want those colours in both bright and pale shades. You may not always want to paint with the most vibrant hues, but you certainly want those intense colours available for when your life warrants them.

The same thing applies with your ends values – your feelings. You don't always choose to live in a state of high passion or excitation, but you want to be able to access your passion at will, especially during those times when you need to act powerfully and confidently to get the result you want. Passion is your key to intensity, to extreme confidence when that's what you need. Finding it and gaining access to it are what this chapter is about.

Discovering Your Passionate Self

Take a moment to recall the last time your heart ached for something. Did you find the energy it brought you empowering? Did you surprise yourself and achieve the outcome you felt so passionate about? Could you have achieved this level of confident action without the passion?

People of Anglo-Saxon origin tend to be uncomfortable with powerful emotions, and passion is about as powerful as they get. Including passionate sexuality (which can often give rise to all manner of problems), passion is most likely to be associated for them with negative outcomes and emotions such as revenge, jealousy, and hatred. This association is a great pity because adopting this narrow view of passion cuts you off from one of your most powerful emotional drivers.

If you're committed to confident living and to getting as much as you can out of each day, passion is an essential emotion in your armoury. With passion, you can take on bigger challenges and achieve greater results in the world.

But while a part of you longs for access to the more vital and more passionate parts of your nature, another part of you is wary of living without holding back. You're probably afraid of making mistakes, of not looking good, of being shown up or otherwise embarrassed by trying too hard and falling flat, and you hold back to avoid such embarrassment.

Holding back becomes a habit and avoiding embarrassment becomes self-defeating as you lose access to the power of your passion. You can experience this holding back as a dramatic loss of confidence and self-belief. Even worse, the bottled-up emotion you're avoiding or denying has a nasty way of biting you back in the form of physical illness or mental breakdown. A better move by far is to take on this rich opportunity to extend your emotional range and embrace passion as one of your most powerful expressions of your being in the world.

Passion is an emotional intensity; a charged-up version of excitement; a supercharged motivation. Passion is a tremendous force that can meet almost any challenge head on. Passion is nature's way of giving you the confidence you need to achieve an outcome that you care deeply about. You can't do without it, so understanding your passionate side and finding out how to use it is well worth your while.

Becoming more passionate

You've the same capacity for passion as any artist, orator, or athlete (or any other group noted for their passion). What you may also have is a series of blockages that stifle your natural passion for living and make it difficult for you to unleash your most passionate self into the world.

To unblock yourself and let your passion flow (something you'll be doing as you study other chapters of this book), you need to open up your heart a little to counter the voices in your head that tell you what you *should* be doing. What this really means is that you need to understand and embrace your *ends values,* the feelings you most want in life, and start to give them the priority they deserve (Chapter 5 explains how you can do this).

Nothing is more important to you right now than the way you *feel.* How you feel dictates the meaning you make of the things happening to you and determines what you do about them.

The feelings you most want in your life can be a reliable guide to what is most appropriate for you. And, provided you then act in accordance with these feelings, you begin to unlock your blocked passion. Robert Dilts, the American psychologist who developed the model of neurological levels we explain in the next section, calls acting in accordance with your feelings *congruence,* which is a powerful idea.

Exploring your neurological levels with Robert Dilts

Being guided by your feelings alone can be a bit like being a castaway on a desert island – it can be beautiful, idyllic even, but unless your experience is also purposeful, meaningful, and engaging, the experience pales and fades with time and may even end in disaster. You need a consistent purpose; and for a confident, powerful, passionate life you need a big purpose – one bigger perhaps than you can realistically expect to be able to fulfil in only one lifetime.

To help you to understand congruence of feelings, thoughts, and actions, and to develop it, you can use Dilts's *neurological levels* – a difficult name for a simple and powerful way of looking at how human beings operate in the world (Kate's book, *Neuro-linguistic Programming For Dummies,* published by Wiley, covers neurological levels in more depth).

Looking at the levels

Dilts believes that you experience yourself in the world at six increasingly powerful but distinct levels. These levels combine to make up your complete human experience.

Following is a description of the levels, and how you usually experience them:

- ✔ **Environment:** The *environment* is your experience of where you live and work, with whom, the prevailing culture, and how things get done. You co-create these environments with other people by the way you allow them to be and the way you interact within them.

- ✔ **Behaviour:** One of the most powerful ways you affect your environment is the way you act in it. Often you feel totally in control of what you do. Sometimes, though, things can get unpredictable, including the way you act and react to events.

- ✔ **Capability:** Living demands a high degree of capability. You have to communicate, and you need to develop social and economic skills. You have to predict how others are going to behave and accommodate your predictions in your interactions with them.

- ✔ **Values and beliefs:** In their purest form, your *values* are the emotional states you want to feel. *Beliefs* are a sense of certainty, your rules of thumb about what feelings to have. They let you make fast decisions but, unquestioned, they may trap you in the past.

- ✔ **Identity:** Your *identity* is your holistic sense of who you are. It rolls up your perception of your environment, behaviour, capabilities, values, and beliefs into a whole, allowing you to relate to the larger systems of work, family, and nation.

- ✔ **Ontology or spirit:** Your *ontology* or *spirit* is your ultimate organising level of experience, including your sense of why you're here and what you're here to do. It may be clear to you, or unclear. Many religious and personal development techniques attempt to expand your sense of self at this level.

You can consider these six levels as your self-structure, or your total sense of *being* in the world. However, the levels are self-contained in a way that leaves room for them to become misaligned. When this happens, you become *incongruent*, leading you to lose your natural confidence to be passionate and take decisive action. To be truly confident and powerful, you need to achieve a high degree of congruence throughout the levels (they need to support and reinforce each other and not conflict). When you achieve this, all these elements of your being combine harmoniously to take you in the same direction.

This fully congruent version of yourself is the awesome version you feel in flashes on the inside but often struggle to present consistently on the outside. Becoming more congruent is your key to personal power and your ticket to total self-confidence.

Exposing your levels

In this section, you use the Dilts model to work out what you know and feel to be true about yourself, and how far you act in accordance with your feelings. Write a simple paragraph about your experience of life from each of the six levels starting with your environment and working up to your spirit. When you've done this, write out a separate description of your experience of the six levels *as you would like each to be*, only this time start with spirit and work down to environment.

By completing your own personal analyses, you get a new sense of how closely your life today compares with how you would like it to be. You can then use the gaps to set up change goals for yourself. Use Nigel's analysis, shown in Figures 7-1 and 7-2, as an example.

Don't be surprised by the degree of congruence you're already achieving in life. You've immense capabilities and power that you take entirely for granted. You may be less surprised by the areas that need your attention, so take a look now at anything in your model that you know is a problem and take steps to resolve it as Nigel does. Nigel's initial self analysis is shown in Figure 7-1.

Analysis of My Levels

Environment – I live with my wife and our four children. We live on the edge of the green belt outside a large city giving me easy access to work and providing a nice country life for my family. I'm in professional services and I serve some of the world's biggest corporations. I don't always support their trading policies, nor the products they create, but the people are usually really great to work with, fair, and decent. I am well paid and this provides private education for the kids and a provision for our life-style and old age.

Behaviour – I think of myself as an easygoing guy, preferring professional behaviour where everyone gets on with things and doesn't require close supervision. I am embarrassed sometimes by the need to correct people at work, and I'm not very good at it. At home I prefer to avoid difficult situations with neighbours, which makes me a little reserved. I guess some people find me standoffish, though I'm not really.

Capability – I am educated to degree level and have worked in my industry over 10 years. I am well known for an original line of analysis and have an established and faithful client base. I have an enquiring mind and a good track record in innovation, often beating my younger colleagues in coming up with powerful new ideas and implementing them. At home I'm not much of a handyman, but I consider myself to be a patient husband and a skilled and loving father to my four children.

Values and Beliefs – I was brought up in the 1960s and 1970s when we thought we could change the world through free thinking and challenging the status quo. I value my free thinking more than almost anything and am disturbed when I see its lack in others. I worry about the world today and see little evidence of the 'better tomorrow' we thought we were building. My liberal politics seem to be falling out of favour again after a brief resurgence in the 1990s. We are destroying the planet and there seems little political will to do anything about it.

Identity – although I no longer worry about being 'found out', I do still feel a bit of an impostor sometimes. I have enjoyed a successful business career without feeling I fully belonged in it. I have worked successfully with people whose values are very different from mine. I feel I have been out of touch with the real me for long periods and have tended to define myself by what I am not and what I don't want rather than what I am and what I stand for.

Ontology or Spirit – I feel like a caged spirit. Who knows what my life would have been like if I had accepted my calling in my 20s instead of selling out to a business career? I have encouraged my children to follow their passions and I've given them permission to think for themselves. Perhaps now, relatively late in life, I can finally fulfill my destiny and contribute to the wellbeing of the planet through responding to my sense of calling.

Figure 7-1: Nigel's analysis of his six levels today.

Nigel's experience of himself at the six neurological levels is distorted by how he feels right now and by pent up emotions such as regret, guilt, and frustration. On the outside he looks to be a highly successful businessman, but he clearly feels he has given up a lot to achieve this.

He now has the opportunity to re-experience himself as he would like to be at the six levels. This time, the instruction is to do it top-down starting with ontology. Nigel's view of himself in Figure 7-2 is aspirational – it doesn't exactly reflect what he feels today, but is still recognisably Nigel and is within his sense of what is possible for himself.

In contrast to Figure 7-1, Nigel's new description of how he wants his levels to be is much more congruent. Much of what he is saying he wants, he has already; he just isn't experiencing it that way. Other things that he can easily do, or emphasise, come to mind as he thinks about how he wants things to be. He now has an aspirational target for change.

To unlock your true passionate self, you need to address those uncomfortable inconsistencies you've been ignoring. If you do this, you transform your experience of life.

Tapping into your natural passion

Perhaps the fastest way to unlock your natural passion is to become clear on what you want, why you want it, and what you can do to get it. The philosopher Friedrich Nietzsche said, 'If a person has a why to live, he can handle almost any what!'

So *why* do you want whatever you've decided you want? Does it support your values? Is what you want consistent with your sense of who you are? Is it worthy of someone put here to do what you've decided you've been put here to do? Are the actions you need to take appropriate to a person with your beliefs and values? Do they support or undermine your sense of who you are? Would you be proud to read about them in the newspaper? Would you want your mother to know about them?

Aspirational Re-Alignment of Neurological Levels

Ontology or Spirit – I have always felt a deep and profound sense of connection to the universe, to nature and to the planet. I feel the need to live in harmony with the planet, including its ecology and its entire people. I feel I was put here to represent the holistic viewpoint and was meant to express it in the world, to my fellow man, to business and to our youth. I would not describe myself as religious, though I have tried various religious paths. My path is pure, free spirit, respect for all and personal responsibility for our individual decisions and contribution.

Identity – who I am, is the embodiment of freedom, tolerance and respect for all. I choose to be an example of an educated, enlightened businessman. When I am at my best I feel supported by an invisible force of nature, a force that orders the world and keeps me honest. I am clear on my roles and contribution and choose them with care. I am reliable: I will always deliver what I have promised. Others see me as a role model, as an inspiration and as a force for good in the world.

Values and Beliefs – I accept and respect the need for commercial integrity, financial propriety, and profit – but profit is not the only important thing in business and I would never put it before people, or before honesty and integrity. I believe there is an order in nature and through the universe, caused by forces we do not fully comprehend. I believe that the good we do in the world comes back to support us in so many ways we are not always aware of. The most important thing in life is the freedom to become who we were meant to become.

Capability – I am a skilled student of life with a commitment to lifetime learning. I am a skilled businessman with a rich and varied experience. I am a skilled speaker and teacher with a keen interest in others' learning. I have vision, passion and energy. I can become excited by new possibilities and I have the passion to enthuse and enroll others into their causes. I am a loving and committed father, and partner to my wife. I can do anything I need to do to fulfill a cause I have taken up.

Behaviour – I am calm and reasoned. I am focused and dedicated to my tasks. I am convivial and respectful of others (but not at the expense of doing a good job or achieving some other committed undertaking). I prefer to live and let-live but I can also be assertive and have no issues with taking stands, of even being one against a crowd when I believe it is warranted. I consistently go with my beliefs and values, people know this about me and don't expect me to do otherwise.

Environment – I prefer to live in situations of calmness and order, where objectives are clear and outcomes are agreed. I choose to be with people who tend to be the same as myself, and in any case accept me the way I am. When disagreements arise, they are resolved before they develop into conflicts and enmities. I operate in successful businesses where people know what I stand for and what I can deliver and they value my contribution.

Figure 7-2: Nigel's analysis of his preferred six levels.

If you answer 'no' to any of the preceding questions, you're sapping your capacity for passion; you're draining it away just as surely as trying to fill up the bath with the plug out. Here are some more drainers to avoid:

✔ **Fear:** *Fear* is the opposite of confidence. This book is full of recipes you can use to help banish it for good.

✔ **Doubt:** *Doubt* comes when you do not know why you're pursuing a certain course of action. You need to be clear and you need a big enough reason to get it done.

✔ **Risk-aversion:** *Risk-aversion* is another manifestation of fear. Don't view risk as something to be avoided; rather see it as something to be managed.

✔ **Procrastination:** *Procrastination* is when you put off doing tough things to make life more pleasant, but it always does the opposite. Get into the habit of doing the tougher things on your list first. This action releases your passion for doing the rest. (If procrastination is a particular problem for you, check out the more detailed analysis of it in Chapter 8).

Being passionate and powerful come naturally to you when you engage with the world over something you care deeply about. The magic key to more passion is more caring. Think through what you want in life, and why you want it. Then use the tools in this book to act more confidently to achieve your goals.

Realising your dreams

Dreams can be a good way to connect to your passion – both sleep dreams and daydreams. Sigmund Freud famously ascribed the cause of dreams to unfulfilled desires, and the dreams themselves to wish fulfilment. It seems that deep longings must find a way into our consciousness if we are to be healthy.

But dreams are not all equal. You can have big dreams and small ones; dreams that are worthy of a life being well lived and others that are less worthy compared with your goals and values. You must always choose whether your dreams merit the resources, energy, and time you must put into fulfilling them.

In today's consumer society, you're bombarded by sophisticated propaganda designed by experts to implant dreams and desires you didn't have before. These manufactured dreams are so powerful that it can be difficult to distinguish what you truly want from what you think you want in the moment only.

The response of many people to all this propaganda is to succumb to the consumer pressure (and very often get themselves into debt), or to resist it, switch off, and, so far as they're able, refuse to play the game. It makes no difference which camp you're in; the result is the same: You all too easily lose touch with what you truly desire and with what brings you fulfilment.

You can achieve the kind of dream that supports the growth of your confidence and power in the world from doing the work in this and other chapters, which are designed to help you understand how you want your life to *be,* and by worrying less about all the stuff you want your life to *have.* If, like wealthy celebrities, you can have pretty much anything you want, instantly, ask what this materialism does to your life. Does it bring you fulfilment? Patently not, if you believe the newspapers.

When you pursue your dreams of *being,* you start on a journey to become all you want to be and more. When you dream of *having,* you lose touch with the person you're becoming in the process of getting the things you're pursuing. You become as Faust in the legend, who traded his soul for the prize he sought.

Putting Your Passion into Action

Evidence suggests that it is realistic to expect an ordinary person to have big dreams and to live them: books, films, and newspapers are full of stories about people who have done exactly that, often producing the most incredible results. But in a way, this is missing the point.

Any life, when carefully enough examined, contains all the ingredients of the epics we all read since childhood. One of the 20th century's greatest novels, *Ulysses* by James Joyce, dissects one 24-hour day of its ordinary hero, Leopold Bloom. In doing so, Joyce shows how this one day contains all the drama and heroism of Homer's original epic about the journey of the Greek hero Ulysses.

Your life, too, is an heroic enterprise, and you're living through it every day. You don't have to make it anything that it isn't already. What you may choose to do is to become more aware of what is really going on for you and give yourself more experience of what you most want. You may even choose to become the confident hero of your heroic enterprise, the hero of your own life. What a thought!

Starting your journey

Your own life is already your hero's journey, but in all probability you're sleepwalking through it with most of your emotions well buttoned down – most people are. Here and now you've the opportunity to wake up! If your life is destined to be a journey, why not make it more of an epic?

If you want to live more intensely every day, begin to become more absorbed by your life by viewing it as an epic adventure. You're obviously the central character, but other heroes surround you playing large and small parts in your story. Their heroism is revealed by their character, and by your attention to the detail of what is really going on in the story.

Joseph Campbell described the fundamental steps of the hero's journey, which you can use here to think through the key stages of your own life adventure. Assume that whatever you choose to do, you will ultimately succeed. Like our heroine, Jan, in the exercise below, if you don't give up, you simply cannot fail.

1. **Accept your calling.**

   What is your sense of what you're here to achieve? This calling may have emerged when you were thinking about your neurological levels in the earlier sections in this chapter. Your calling can be a major sense of vocation or simply something you dream about.

If you've no clear ideas, imagine yourself in your healthy old age telling the gathering of your clan the story of your wonderful life, and just make it up. Your journey will contain many twists and turns anyway, so make a start and trust that your calling becomes clearer. By accepting a calling, you're confronting your limitations and breaking through them.

Jan is a nurse who serves as an example for this exercise. She had always wanted to be a nurse, but her experience of nursing in the NHS didn't match up to her expectations. Long hours of heavy and often menial work left her exhausted with little of the satisfaction she expected from helping sick people recover their health. She decided from this point to see herself on a hero's journey and to respond to her calling in a more positive way.

2. **Cross the threshold.**

Do whatever you have to do to summon up the confidence to take that first step. In stepping out, you're immediately in new territory that your old maps don't cover and where your past experience may not help you. Have confidence that you're able to rise to new challenges as they come up with new solutions you develop to fit the situation.

Jan confronted the idea of quitting nursing to retrain for some other profession. But she couldn't imagine giving up on her dream of helping others. Instead, she decided to take on further training to become a more specialised and more valuable nurse – to go forward into growth and not backward into fear.

3. **Find a guardian and face your demons.**

The saying goes: 'When the student is ready, the teacher will appear.' Having stepped out, you're in a position to find the guidance and sponsorship you need. Trust that this help will be there and be sensitive to the guidance that comes your way.

Realise that demons aren't necessarily bad or evil, they're just energy (inner fears, competitors, crises). To move beyond their influence, you have to face them and remove their hold over you.

Jan now began to seek advice. A friend asked her what she most loved about nursing, and what she would miss most if she gave it up. She began to realise that it was the impact she could have on families that was most important to her, especially dealing with mothers. She decided to specialise in women's health and in family management.

But this decision meant going back to school for more formal training, and she had struggled to pass all of her nursing exams in the first place. Was there a way around this? No. In the end she had to weigh up the consequences of not going back to college and, with her husband's pledge of support, she decided to give it a go.

4. **Transform the demons and complete your mission.**

   Your defeated demons can become resources you can use on your journey. This may be in the form of new skills, resources, or tools that enable you to fulfil your calling.

   In fulfilling your calling and completing your mission, you create a new and bigger world to live in, and a new map by which to navigate. These incorporate the growth and discoveries your journey has provided for you.

   As a mature student, Jan found college a different experience from her first time. She was much more focused on what she had to learn and get done. She tackled her assignments early and usually managed to get things in on time.

   Still, the exams were always going to be the big trial. When they came around though, she was well prepared and wasn't fazed as much as she had feared. She was even able to help several of the younger students, who weren't so well prepared, through their ordeal. She passed with distinction, an experience that transformed her beliefs about her capabilities and her fear of exams.

5. **Find your way home.**

   You're now living your life at a higher level. In finding your way home, you're able to share your discoveries and experiences with your loved ones and pave the way for others to follow their dreams and embark on their own hero's journeys.

Even with the new qualifications, it took a while for Jan to find exactly the role she wanted, but she found it eventually in a local community health centre. After she settled in, her new boss shared with her why she had been the preferred candidate. It was because there was something special about the way she carried herself. Even though other candidates were even better qualified, Jan had impressed with her presence, her maturity, and her confidence. It was as though 'she knew what she wanted' and the health centre was proud to have been chosen by her!

You can build these classical elements of the journey into your day, your week, your month, and your lifetime. You're in command of all of this, so take control. Make the journey of your life equal to the power, passion, and confidence you have at your disposal.

Sit with these ideas for a while and reconnect with some of the aspirations of the younger you. What would this level of desire bring to your life today? Do you have a sense of calling? Do you feel deep down that you aren't living the life you're meant to lead? What will happen if you change things? You can. Allow yourself to believe and use this belief to access your passionate self. What may happen if you do? How will the world be changed?

Using your passion to lead

The British Prime Minister and statesman, Harold MacMillan, said in the 1960s that the world needed a theme. Back in his day, with Europe recovering from the Second World War and the standoff of the Cold War well entrenched, this statement may have been true, but not today. In today's world, great global themes unite all of humankind, but true leadership is still hard to find.

What the world needs now is leadership at all levels; and this leadership includes you. Whatever the scale of your ambition, why else do you want to become more confident if not to be more influential in the world and better able to lead others with your vision of the way things should be? Why else would we write this book to enable you to bring the most confident version of yourself into the world?

At whatever level you choose to engage, you need passion to lead.

In business, character-based leadership is a hot topic. Many have finally woken up to the fact that leadership is about leading people – people with ordinary lives but sometimes exceptional hopes, dreams, and aspirations. Leaders who are able to help us to connect to and realise our dreams can achieve extraordinary new levels of performance. But no gimmicks can achieve this, only authentic (no pretence), honest-to-goodness character.

Warren Bennis, the world's leading authority on character-based leadership, says that the process of becoming a leader is not very different from that of becoming an integrated human being. A great leader then, is an integrated human being on a great mission, on a great journey to a better future.

If you've done the work in this chapter, you are this person and your destiny is leadership. Don't fear it, take it on. Leadership is the ultimate destiny of your passionate, powerful, and confident self – the self you're creating.

Part III

Building Your Confident Self

The 5th Wave   By Rich Tennant

"We're looking for someone with a high level of self confidence, Mr. Anthony. Unfortunately, I think you're over qualified."

In this part . . .

A key insight in this part is that you need to forget being perfect if you want to be most effective – the 80/20 rule comes into play. You discover that you operate at your peak by paying attention to how your mind and body connect and find out how to make that connection. Here, you discover your powerful voice and practise the Guaranteed Success Formula as a fool-proof approach for getting results.

Chapter 8

Moving Beyond Perfection

● ●

In This Chapter

▶ Freeing yourself from the perfection pressure

▶ Finding your own way of living happily

▶ Banishing procrastination

▶ Taking things one step at a time

▶ Getting realistic

● ●

A state of perfection in life may be the ideal to attain, but attaining and holding perfection is quite simply impossible. In fact, striving to do so damages your confidence because you will consistently fail to keep up your standard. In any case, is there any fun in being perfect? Being with 'perfect' people can be horribly boring! So in this chapter, we look at how you can be the best you can be, but without driving yourself insane or collapsing under the stress of trying too hard.

Keep in mind that you're a human being; you're not some sort of superhero. As a human being, you're already perfectly fine and doing your best. So as you travel through the next few pages, chuck out your 'perfect expert who must be in control of life' view of yourself and adopt a simpler, more philosophical way to move on. Already, you and those around you are doing the best you can, and your best will get better as you gain more knowledge.

Letting Go of Unreal Expectations

The poet Robert Browning said: 'A man's reach should be beyond his grasp, or what's a heaven for.' Having goals and dreams, the things you're going towards in your life, is wonderful, and we fully encourage you to aim for the stars. Yet there may be times when the goals you set, and the speed at which you want to attain them, put you under really crazy pressure. It's like expecting to be the British Prime Minister or the next President of the USA when actually becoming a local councillor or standing as candidate for your favourite political party is a more than acceptable step on the success ladder. You may find you have more practical impact in your community and a better quality of life at a less senior level.

In moving forward, you may want to keep your sights closer to home too.

Admitting that you can't be perfect (and that you don't want to be)

Liz grew up as the only child of parents who adored her. They told her she was perfect – beautiful, talented, and able to do anything she set her mind to. Yet the continual pressure on her to be top of the class, the most popular student, as well as good looking and slender became a burden as she hit her thirties. She suffered from stress-related illnesses that affected her job as a project manager for an international firm.

Expecting perfection from yourself brings problems and knocks to your confidence: one is that you make unfavourable comparisons with other people all the time; another is that you set yourself on a pedestal that's all too fragile. Being on top of the pedestal at all times isn't a healthy place to be because you never have a chance to recharge your batteries and soon wear yourself down. It's like being a pop star on tour all year, or a perpetually flowering plant. You never get a chance to just chill out if you're constantly looking for the next achievement.

Similarly, being regarded as the expert in your field is good for your ego and confidence in one way, but it can also be a lonely position that alienates you from the rest of the team or organisation and puts you under huge pressure to solve problems single-handedly.

You may wonder how to overcome perfection pressure. Our strategy as coaches is to step off the perfection pedestal. We prefer to listen to our clients, ask questions and free people to find answers without putting themselves under pressure. In this way, we build on the client's innate strength.

Think about an area – at work or home – in which you're trying to be perfect. Now acknowledge that you can't be perfect and let the pressure roll off your back. Feel it go and gently land at your feet. That's better.

Focusing on perfection distracts you from excellence

Instead of 'perfection', try adopting 'excellence' as a more useful objective. When you aim for excellence, you simply go for the best, aiming high and accepting that there will be times when you don't quite reach the summit. Substituting excellence for perfection doesn't mean you don't have high standards and expectations – you do. But it does mean you can be easier on yourself and in so doing you're more likely to succeed in what you really want to achieve, and thus boost your confidence.

How can you develop excellence? Think of an area of your life that's important to you. Maybe you'd like to create a happy relationship with someone significant. How will you know when you've got it? Picture what it will be like when you succeed, what you see yourself doing, saying and feeling. Make a note of it now and write it in the present tense to make it more real for yourself. For example: 'I have a wonderful relationship with this person and I prefer to spend my time with her to being with anyone else. We have fun when we go out together and enjoy quiet evenings at home in each other's company. I am telling her that I care about her and I have a sense of contentment just being close to her.'

Getting clear about what you want puts you on the way to achieving it.

Turning perfection into an excuse

John had a dream to move house in his retirement and live by the sea. He shared it with his new partner Juanita. She was inspired by the idea – she too had always wanted to live by the sea.

John spent two years taking Juanita on 'away days' around estate agents in English seaside resorts looking for the perfect house to move to. Unfortunately, every house that she thought was great, he found something wrong with. His requirements for the perfect house and location became increasingly stringent and uncompromising. He gave up the dream as an impossible move.

Meanwhile, Juanita set off on her own, sold her flat in the North, and moved to one in a pleasant small town on the South Coast. Now she is happy to walk along the beach every day or cycle along the promenade and take in the sea air and her new-found feeling of freedom. The flat is excellent without being perfect. She's living the life she dreamed of while John remains on a never-ending search for perfection.

Being Generous to Yourself First

In order to support other people, be generous to yourself too. Many people run ragged putting themselves after everybody else, including their mother-in-law's dog. The result? Confidence drops and resentment builds, alongside ill health and unhappy relationships.

Practise being generous to yourself – give yourself the unconditional love of a parent for a child. Make time each day to be alone, even if only for ten minutes.

When considering the requests on your time, ask yourself: What does this activity do for me? Does it fit with my agenda, priorities and values? Politely let go of others' demands, pressures, needs, and perceptions. You have needs too, which are just as important.

Acknowledging your successes

Jonnie is a learning junkie. He's taken several degree and postgraduate courses and a vast array of private courses – everything from garden design and photography to software programming and business negotiation. His cupboards are stashed full of manuals, CD learning sets, and certificates. Yet he's so caught up in courses that he never has time to apply what he's found out, and in every new project he compares himself to the specialists in that field.

If you ever catch yourself running so fast through everyday life that you forget to stop and realise what you're discovering and achieving, a 'done it, toss it over the shoulder' mentality is at work. When you're always looking to the future rather than the here and now, you tend to notice what hasn't happened and what you haven't done rather than what you've already completed. You may be piling the pressure on yourself to do more, and your to-do lists become longer and longer. Even holidays become packed itineraries. Such competitive pressure zaps your confidence.

For your sanity, pay attention to what you've achieved rather than just pushing yourself harder. So, look back over the last year and acknowledge your accomplishments and successes:

1. **Put on your success sunglasses and take out a large piece of blank paper.**
2. **Write down every success you can think of.**

   What new things have you found out? What relationships have you nurtured? How has your life moved on in some way?

   Acknowledge the everyday successes as well the big ones. Perhaps you've nursed someone through an illness, supported a friend, or completed a course of study. Perhaps you discovered the importance of time to chill out. Maybe you joined a new team at work or prepared food 365 days of the year for your family. Don't forget to count the money you raised for a charity or the jumble sales you supported at your kids' school.

3. **Keep writing until your blank page is full.**

4. **Now sit back and give yourself a pat on the back.**

    Well done. You're already a success.

At any point when your confidence dives, just take a look at your success list – remind yourself of how much you've achieved to keep positive.

Accepting help and delegating

To recognise that you can't do everything yourself all the time and to let some things go takes confidence. So how about relinquishing control and asking for help? For example, to succeed at work, you need to let go of tasks that you can perform in order to develop those people who report to you and get them to share in the load. Likewise at home, allow your partner to take their share of the tasks, even if they don't do it in quite the same way as you'd like.

 In a work or home context, list the tasks you find most time consuming or burdensome (for example, updating the customer database at work or doing the laundry at home). Ask yourself:

- ✔ What would I most like to have help with or delegate to others?

- ✔ Who can help me and what's the benefit or reward for them?

- ✔ Putting time and money to one side for now, what's really stopping me accepting help and delegating?

- ✔ What will I do to get help? And when?

Whenever you're feeling overloaded, go back to your list and find something to delegate. You'll find the lighter load so much easier.

I am enough

One of our favourite stories on letting go of perfection is told in Naomi Remen's *The Search for Healing*, about her experience of attending a seminar given by the therapist Carl Rogers.

In the seminar, Rogers tried to analyse what he did as a therapist by giving a demonstration of unconditional positive regard in a client therapeutic session. He said: 'I realise there's something I do before I start a session. I let myself know that I am enough. Not perfect. Perfect wouldn't be enough. But that I am human, and that is enough. There is nothing this man can say or do or feel that I can't feel in myself. I can be with him. I am enough.'

Remen was stunned by this speech and says: 'I felt as if some old wound in me, some fear of not being good enough, had come to an end. I knew inside myself that what he had said was absolutely true: I am not perfect, but I am enough.'

Overcoming Procrastination

Question: What's your procrastination all about?

Answer: I don't know. Can I tell you later?

If confidence is about focusing your energy and acting decisively, then procrastination is the direct opposite. *Procrastination* scatters your energy and puts off acting at all – sometimes you avoid even deciding. You postpone and postpone. You dither about. Perhaps you've a proposal or essay to write and you keep putting it off and finding excuses for inactivity. Maybe you've a tax form to fill out, the cupboard to tidy, the difficult phone call to make, the button to sew on, the cobwebs to dust off the ceiling, or the medical check-up. It – whatever the current 'it' happens to be – never happens.

Unless you're hyper-organised, you probably have something sitting on a 'to do' list that hasn't become urgent enough yet to do something about it. If so, you're qualified to join the procrastination club – if only club members can get a date and venue organised to meet up. Maybe next week.

Procrastination is the ultimate waiting game: waiting for someone else to take the lead; waiting for something else to happen first; and above all waiting for everything to be perfect before you do anything. Procrastination comes when you lack focus and energy. When you're high on focus and energy, the positive result you get is purposeful action.

The quick secret to bust through procrastination is to do something, anything, but just get moving. As writers we face the blank page each day. So we start writing anything, even if when the first draft is pure rubbish.

In the next sections, we look at practical ideas to allow you to break through procrastination. Confidence requires action and the mind-set to keep on your front foot.

Breaking the gridlock

Clients often come to coaching because they're stuck in what we call the *X then Y gridlock* scenario. They've a goal, a dream, something they want to realise, and yet they're not doing it. Instead, the conversation is around: 'I can't do X until Y.' These messages are the kind we hear that signify people are putting their lives on hold. Some may be familiar to you:

'I can't do the training course until the children are older.'

'I can't turn professional until I have sponsorship.'

'I can't travel to Australia until my health is better.'

'I can't leave/change my job until my partner's business has taken off.'

'I can't buy my cottage house by the sea until I'm rich.'

'I can't get to the gym until I change jobs, and I can't change jobs until my partner finds a higher-paying job. . .'

'I can't lose weight until my wife stops cooking delicious dinners every night.'

. . . and on it goes. The treacle gets stickier by the day. This stuck situation becomes debilitating, and reduces both energy and confidence.

In order to achieve a big dream, most people quite rightly argue that not having enough time, money, or energy limits them. However, these aren't the sole reasons why people get stuck. Essentially, they struggle because they haven't broken a large job into steps.

Try this step-by-step approach to breaking the pattern of gridlock for yourself and for others.

1. **Put aside the idea that you don't have enough time, money, or energy – assume the lack of any or all these elements is not the real problem.**

   Imagine that you're rich enough in time, money, or energy.

2. **State your goal or dream in a positive way and write it down.**

   For example: 'I want to move to a cottage by the sea.'

3. **Ask yourself Question 1: 'Can I do it today?'**

   If your answer is yes, everything is in place, hey presto your dream is complete. However, if your answer is no – and this is the most likely scenario – then proceed to Step 4.

4. **Ask yourself Question 2: 'What needs to happen first?'**

   Break out all the separate tasks you need to do to accomplish your goal.

   In the example of the house by the sea, the tasks can divide into three main activities: researching the location, finding a more flexible job, and getting the family's agreement.

5. **Loop around the questions in Steps 3 and 4 for each task.**

   Ask yourself Question 1, 'Can I do it today?' and if not, then Question 2, 'What needs to happen first?', until you arrive at a list of activities that you can do today or you've negotiated with yourself to do on a set date that you write in your diary.

Get the idea? In this way, you've broken through the gridlock, and are moving towards your dream.

Biting off smaller chunks

Patience and persistence are valuable qualities to help build your confidence. And when you calmly stick at things, breaking large tasks into smaller ones, you're more likely to get closer to perfection than if you rush at a job looking for a quick fix.

Bob calmly tackles stressful challenges in his job in a global IT team as well as in his hobbies by keeping his cool and seeing large projects as simply a collection of smaller chunks. At work, his job is to help transform the efficiency of an international airline – a seemingly impossible task. Yet he breaks things down into a series of smaller and smaller chunks. First he identifies the critical business processes, then maps business processes onto the existing IT infrastructure. From there he looks at process performance measures, identifies issues and resources, and sets up smaller projects to tackle improvements that make a difference.

At home, Bob takes a similar approach to large challenges, whether he's building a garden, renovating the house, or flying a glider. When he first decided he wanted to find out how to fly, he did his research, found a gliding club, booked on a beginners' course, and set himself a series of challenges that he has quietly ticked off one by one: flying solo, flying a single-seater glider, an endurance flight, a long cross-country flight. None of these has required any great fuss, as his practical approach is just to 'get on and have a go', knowing that he will gain confidence as he finds out more.

In order to break your own projects into smaller chunks, follow these steps:

1. **Set your big goal.**

   For example, perhaps you want to write a novel.

2. **Set a reasonable and realistic timeframe.**

   Writing a novel may take a year.

3. **Break your goal down into a series of small activities to accomplish within the timeframe.**

For writing a novel, these activities may include finding a publisher, firming up the story line, and developing your creative writing skills.

4. **Set specific timeframes for each activity.**

   Each novel-writing activity may take several months of work to complete.

5. **Break each activity into a series of daily habits or short projects.**

   So, developing your creative writing skills may translate to new habits such as attending a creative writing evening class each week and writing for an hour each day.

Organising a project into manageable tasks lets you tackle the largest task with confidence.

Taking Time Off – For You

All work and no play makes for a dull life. It's also highly unproductive. If you stay at work for crazy hours, you know how your productivity dips quickly after the main shift.

If you wonder what it would be like to slow down a bit and keep things simple, the information in the next sections gives you a glimpse. Notice how, when you slow down, you have a chance to reflect from a position of confidence on what you really want, rather than reacting to other people's needs all of the time.

Slowing down

You may be used to acceleration, working in top gear, tweeting and blogging as you speed from place to place by the fastest route possible and rarely stopping to think. Society today is geared to fast – fast food, fast cars, fast computers, fast results, and instant gratification. 'I want it, and I want it today.'

Yet your moments of inspiration most often come in the quiet moments when you give your brain a chance to unwind a bit: on the day you take off from work; in the shower; on the gym bike; ambling around the park; working in the garden; walking along a country lane. Rarely does your best thinking occur when you're buzzing around like a busy bumble bee in a flower patch.

Your brain may appear to work wonders at speed, yet it works so much better if you give it a chance to relax at regular intervals. Perversely, going slow speeds up the results you get. Take a break, a complete break, and you come back refreshed. Neuroscientists are increasingly providing the scientific arguments to back up ideas that meditators have promoted for centuries: that the brain works most efficiently when you give it periods of rest from high-pressure activities.

Meditation offers a calm sea to support you in negotiating the choppy moments in life. That's why millions of people around the world now practise meditation each day.

Here's a two-minute meditation you can do yourself before an important meeting or before the baby awakes – whenever you'd like to slow down gently and savour time for yourself. You may like to read it out aloud slowly to yourself or record your voice saying it and listen to the recording. Let your mind be free . . . free of any thoughts or worries. Let them go. Allow them to float away gently on the breeze. Take your awareness to your breathing. Simply notice as it rises and falls gracefully in your chest and abdomen, with no comment from the mind. Allow your thoughts to come . . . and then to go. Observe the colours and pictures around you, take in the light, and bathe your body and mind in its generous warmth. Hear the sounds in the room and beyond. Let them soften to the furthest corners of your mind, then let them go. Feel the movement of the air on your face and on your body, and bask in that cool stillness. Smell . . . taste the delicacy of the silence. Rest in that calm awareness for a few moments. And when you're ready, come back to now – refreshed, energised, and ready to move on.

Adopting the 80/20 principle

When Kate worked in corporate advertising, she knew the rule that roughly 20 per cent of her advertising spending produced 80 per cent of the results in any campaign. The problem was always to know which 20 per cent was really working. Fortunately, the data is clearer to gather and interpret in other, less fickle areas of life, and we explore the 80/20 principle in the next sections.

Explaining the split

Pareto's law, or the *80/20 principle,* is named after the 19th-century economist Vilfredo Pareto, who discovered that 80 per cent of the land in Italy was owned by 20 per cent of the population. He also, allegedly, noticed in his garden that 80 per cent of the peas he harvested came from 20 per cent of the pea pods.

Over the years, the same generalised principle has been applied to interesting effect in many other areas beyond land ownership and gardening. Most importantly for you, this principle suggests that 80 per cent of your results come from 20 per cent of your effort, and, in turn, it takes the 80 per cent of your remaining resources to shift that extra 20 per cent from 80 per cent to 100 per cent. All of that is good evidence of the real cost of perfection. To squeeze out that extra 20 per cent is going to cost you four times the effort. Some things are worth that effort and some are not.

The 80/20 rule is a rough approximation to what happens in reality, but here are some examples of where you may spot Pareto's law in action:

- ✔ Twenty per cent of your cleaning effort gets 80 per cent of your home sparkling.
- ✔ Twenty per cent of your customers bring in 80 per cent of the sales.
- ✔ Twenty per cent of the people in your office create 80 per cent of the results.
- ✔ Eighty per cent of your progress comes from 20 per cent of the activities on your to-do list.

 ✔ Twenty per cent of your clothes are worn 80 per cent of the time.

 ✔ Twenty per cent of the meeting time results in 80 per cent of the decisions.

Adjusting the split as needed

Recently, a friend was studying for a qualification that involved writing clinical essays. Writing is not her favourite pastime and she became increasing anxious about this piece of work until she decided she could take pressure off herself. 'I'm working on an 80 per cent essay – one good enough to get me the marks I need and still have time for the family and me.'

It was an eminently sensible application of the 80/20 principle – to do her best in the time she had, and then to stop rather than trying to extract the extra marks and suffer unduly in the process.

We believe that busyness is one of the biggest challenges that ordinary folks face. By aiming to do 100 per cent all the time, you dramatically lose energy and focus. If you were to apply the 80/20 rule, you can cut out 80 per cent of your activities and increase your leisure time dramatically.

Identify an area where you're struggling to achieve 100 per cent perfection. Decide on an 80 per cent result that is acceptable to you. Now allocate 20 per cent of your time to focusing on purposefully achieving this result.

Generating Realistic Standards of Behaviour

Perfectionism and procrastination are both ultimately time wasters in most circumstances. They take vast amounts of your energy. Naturally, you want to be your best, and circumstances exist where you're competing to excel and want to give it your 100 per cent. The point is to get real as well as having a vision.

Most successful people recognise the benefit of keeping things simple, as in the famous acronym *KISS – Keep it Simple, Stupid.*

The harder and more complex you make things for yourself, the more you're likely to make a mess when things get too tough, and lose your confidence in your ability to succeed.

Adjusting your goals to the circumstances

The previous section explains how 80 per cent of your results come from 20 per cent of your work. So, in moving towards your own vision and goals, adopting habits that stop your dillydallying procrastination and keep your energy focused is important. Here are some questions to ask yourself as you constantly re-evaluate your route forward.

- ✔ What's the vision now? (And reconnect with why this vision is important for you.)
- ✔ What am I doing that I can delegate to others?
- ✔ What am I doing that doesn't need to be done at all?
- ✔ What can I do that no one else can do to achieve this vision?

Capture your answers and refer to them whenever you need to stay on track. Refer to them at least once every month, and ideally more frequently.

Staying positive while keeping it real

Times and situations will arise when your confidence plummets due to external factors over which you've little or no control. Here are some tips for staying positive and holding it together.

- ✔ Think about a time in the future when none of what is happening now will matter.
- ✔ Plan a series of small treats for yourself, even if some time needs to elapse before you can enjoy them.

✔ Imagine that you're in a movie, and this scene is the bad bit, but you know the movie has a happy ending. Write your own happy ending.

✔ Go to bed early with a hot water bottle.

✔ Eat the best-quality, healthiest food available and drink lots of water.

✔ Take a walk and marvel at the sky, the air, the greenery.

✔ Remember everything that has gone smoothly, however small the event.

✔ List out the things that are perfect about this most difficult situation right now.

Increasing your flexibility

For years, long-distance running was Joanne's favourite exercise and form of stress release. She was part of a close-knit running club, ran several miles before work through all weathers, and enlisted for competitive runs at weekends. Running at speed was a theme for all of her life in the fast lane – a high-powered job as a board director for a large firm with a demanding travel schedule – that she felt she ought to adhere to, in spite of a desire to spend time with her family. Her children rarely saw her, and her husband felt as if he was a single dad much of the time, bringing up the children on his own.

A hamstring injury enforced a break in Joanne's running schedule. On the advice of her physiotherapist, she exchanged her running routine for swimming and yoga practice at home, and clawed back more time to create an attractive environment in the cottage and relax with her husband and children at weekends. The enforced change of routine encouraged Joanne to take stock of her working life and day, and to change from spending time on activities she felt she 'ought to' do to those that she really wanted to do. She realised that she'd been stuck in a rut of the same exercise and mixing with the same group of people.

When she became more flexible in her exercise routine, she allowed more flexibility and space in her life for her family, and redefined her company role in a way that truly fitted for her. Taking this confident action improved her relationships, and her energy soared once more.

Think about your daily and weekly routines with an eye towards looking at areas where you may be stuck with certain habits that do you no favours. Where would some change, however small, have the most impact? Consider the routines you've developed that have become less than inspiring. Do you, for example, always mix with the same people, spend your weekends in the same way each week, or visit the same places time after time?

Examine the things you *always* do, feel you *ought* to do, or *never* do and try something different. Perhaps you've got into a boring rut. If you always eat Sunday lunch with your mother or tackle the housework every Friday morning, experiment by doing something different. What would happen if you took your mother to the beach on Sunday for a picnic or spent Friday morning playing a round of golf?

Flexibility is a route to freedom. The more adaptable you become, the less you're harnessed to the pressure of perfection. In turn, confidence builds.

Chapter 9

Stretching Yourself Mentally

*T*he truth behind the advice 'Enjoy life; this is not a dress rehearsal' underlines the fact that you cannot always prepare for what life throws your way, and if you attempt to insulate yourself from the unexpected, you end up missing out on so much of the richness that life has to offer.

Do you remember the test in the fairytale, *The Princess and the Pea*? To find out whether the visitor is royal, the courtiers trick her into sleeping on a pile of ten mattresses with a simple, garden pea hidden underneath the bottom one. Being an authentic princess, she is unable to sleep due to the discomfort this pea causes her, and next morning she is full of complaints about the lumpy mattresses.

This information is as much as we find out about this princess, but we know from other fairytales that princesses are often unable to eat normal food, are allergic to dust and grime, cannot bear to be questioned or contradicted, are paralysed by the least setback, and their lives seem much less easy than they should be. Despite all their privileges (or because of them), fairytale royalty seems less able to cope with life than simple, ordinary folk.

Like a lot of folk literature, a truth lies at the heart of these princess tales. The tales are about human beings who have shrunk in stature and capabilities because they've never had to stretch to meet a challenge. Facing up to difficulties is one of the most important drivers of all human growth. So, in this chapter, we show you how to embrace the challenges life places your way and use them positively – as stepping stones to achieving your full confidence and power in the world.

Expanding Your Comfort Zone

What we mean by your comfort zone is a lot more than just your physical environment. *Comfort zone,* a term in widespread use in psychology and personal development, mostly refers to aspects of your mental environment, the one you've created for yourself. Think of your comfort zone as your den, the place where you feel truly relaxed just being yourself. This place is familiar territory – easy and comfortable.

You can readily see how even the most comfortable of dens becomes boring and over-restrictive if you never get out of it. But your psychological comfort zone is different from your den at home in one important respect – this zone is slowly shrinking! Unless you take steps to expand it again, your psychological comfort zone will squeeze you to death.

To be a healthy human being, you have to be able to stretch your mental environment from time to time. You grow much more quickly in confidence when you accept your need to expand.

Here's another useful analogy. Imagine yourself lying in bed on a cold and stormy night. Outside the wind is howling and you can hear the rain lashing against the windowpanes. Inside, though, you're cosy and protected under your duvet. As long as you stay put, you *feel* that you can see the storm through in comfort.

But how good a guide are your immediate feelings of comfort? If the storm goes on for a while, you're liable to get hungry, and if the wind takes off your roof, you're going to be extremely uncomfortable and perhaps fall into danger. In these circumstances, your bed isn't going to offer you any real protection, and you need to get out and find a safer place. You won't find your storm cellar so comfortable but you're better off there in a storm. You may want to prepare one.

Comfort is a poor guide in life: an illusion that is entirely subjective and relative to the moment. You may usually baulk at a cold shower, but if you're on a camping safari and the temperature outside is 105 degrees, a cold shower out of a bucket may seem a luxury. Comfort always depends upon context.

Understanding the limits of your zone

Think of your comfort zone as your routine living, working, and social environments; those places, activities, and relationships where you feel most at home. Nothing is wrong with living in this zone most of the time. Doing so makes it possible for you to get through your days without continually having to re-evaluate every nuance of every situation. But, just as your beliefs are decisions about what things mean that can keep you trapped in outmoded thought, so never venturing beyond living within your comfort zone can render you unfit to face the adventure of life.

Just as you need to stretch your body's muscles and ligaments regularly to maintain your physical strength and wellbeing, so you need also to give your mind a stretch to maintain its power and flexibility. Just as you must use your muscles or lose them, so it is with the growth possibilities that life presents to you. You must seize them when you can or settle for living in an ever-shrinking comfort zone that constricts and stifles you, that steals your possibilities for love and joy, and affects your sense of self-confidence.

Everyone has a tendency to avoid painful or potentially difficult situations. However, each time you avoid them, you withdraw a little bit farther into your comfort zone. Unless you deliberately stretch yourself from time to time, you're eventually hiding under the mental equivalent of your duvet with storm demons raging all around you.

The next time you feel awkward or embarrassed and want to withdraw from a situation for no good reason, remember that choosing not to exercise your mental powers – hiding in your comfort zone – is the very opposite of confidence; you need to be on your guard against it. The knowledge you gain from this book can help you break through your limiting beliefs.

Coming alive

In his youth, Mike was a fine athlete. Small in stature, he was nonetheless strong and quick, with a winner's spirit born out of competition with his four brothers. When he was married with children of his own and the responsibilities of a demanding job, his time for sports was squeezed out. When he became responsible for an entire business region in his company, he spent more and more time travelling, both entertaining and being entertained, and living mostly on hotel and restaurant food. He put on weight and began to worry about his physique for the first time in his life.

Another promotion saw him transferred back to head office. When his new team members asked him to make up their numbers in the indoor football tournament, he accepted. But when he went out for a training run with them, he had to work hard to keep up and he didn't enjoy it at all. He missed the other two training sessions due to 'pressure of work', but the truth is that his body was hurting. So he decided that playing would be less arduous than training and he decided to 'wing it'.

On the evening of the tournament, Mike's life changed. He ended up with torn ligaments and a leg broken in several places. Lying in his hospital bed, after the operations, he yearned for the simple pleasure of a walk in the park with his wife, and the time to enjoy it. He knew that his 'accident' could have been so much worse and decided to reappraise his life and work and make changes.

Mike had always gone where the company needed him without question and done what his employer asked. In return, he received regular salary increases, pension rights, a steadily improving company car, and an expense account. What he had lost was his natural affinity for decision making, competition, risk taking, growth, and self-determination. Mike realised that although he enjoyed the trappings of success, he had lost touch with a large part of his physical being. He had lived in a shrinking physical comfort zone for the previous 15 years.

After his recovery, Mike quit his job to set up a small enterprise with his younger brother. They now arrange and lead adventure holidays and corporate leadership safaris. Now Mike's whole life is a stretch and he is fitter in all dimensions. 'I feel like I'm alive again,' he reports. 'I'm enjoying being active, thinking up new ideas, responding to new situations. I never know what next week will bring. My life is an adventure and my work, helping people to break out of their own comfort zones, is a joy.'

Decide now to become more proactive in your family life, work, and other relationships and you can begin to use any small opportunity for growth that presents itself to you. These regular small stretches make you familiar with feeling challenged, and the more familiar you are with a feeling, the less you fear it. When bigger challenges show up in your life, you're in a far better position mentally to take them on.

Stretching your boundaries: Expanding your zone

Just as you may advocate regular visits to the gym and the lifting of light weights that you can gradually increase, so it is with your mental stretching.

If you're terrified of public speaking, for example, it may over-stretch you to lead a funeral oration or to deliver a witty and gracious personal tribute to a beloved boss on her retirement, though you can aspire to these things and easily achieve them over time. Remember, the journey of a thousand miles begins with a single step. The best way to start in public speaking, for example, is to take any small opportunity to speak up in a group, in a routine weekly meeting say, or informal social gathering.

One of the most revealing aspects of the Comfort Zone Theory is that *any* stretch expands your capacity in all areas simultaneously. To examine this point, look at Figure 9-1 and say that you're facing these challenges in the next few months:

- ✔ You put yourself forward for a promotion you feel you've earned and now have the important interview to get through.

- ✔ Your oldest friend is getting married and has asked you to be the Best Man. You felt honoured to accept but now you have to make the dreaded speech.

- ✔ You're attracted to a young lady in Accounts, and she seems to be interested in you too. Your workmates have begun teasing you and putting pressure on you to ask her out.

- ✔ You've a life-long fear of snakes and yet you've agreed to accompany your young nephew, who idolises you, on a visit to a snake farm. This trip will entail handling the snakes, something that fills you with dread.

Figure 9-1: Looking at the comfort zone.

Right now *all* these things are outside your comfort zone. You can see yourself doing the first two, at a stretch, but asking your colleague for a date has you feeling queasy, and you've no idea how to deal with your snake phobia.

The best thing you can do in this situation is to start where you feel the most stuck. By getting help with your snake phobia, you increase your capacity to deal with the other, seemingly unrelated, situations as well. Amazing and true! Think of it as though when you expand your comfort zone in any direction, you expand its radius, bringing many other things within your new, expanded circumference.

Phobias are most easily dealt with through simple therapies such as hypnotherapy or Neuro-linguistic Programming, and if you seek this kind of help you can also address any general anxiety you may have around social situations like speeches, interviews, and asking for dates.

Facing up to anxiety

Faced with something that scares you, or that seems well beyond your present capabilities, you may experience a dry mouth, butterflies in the tummy, knocking knees, and so on. You may refer to these feelings as anxiety, but a better description is apprehension at the prospect of facing something unfamiliar. To feel a little apprehensive when facing a specific, new stretch is normal, and is a good indicator that you're engaging in growth activity. Apprehension is your friend; anxiety is something else.

Anxiety is not related to anything specific at all. Anxiety is a complex combination of fear, apprehension, and dread, often accompanied by physical sensations such as palpitations and shortness of breath. Anxiety is a vague, unpleasant emotion experienced in anticipation of some usually ill-defined misfortune. Because of its vagueness it can interfere with lots of areas of life.

The normal antidote to occasional anxiety is common sense: thinking about your situation in specifics, spelling out your requirements in detail, thinking through your actions carefully. If this approach doesn't bring relief and anxiety and symptoms persist, you may need more specialised help.

Recognising anxiety disorders

Don't confuse a mildly anxious response to a situation you find challenging with a range of more serious anxiety disorders. These conditions can fill people's lives with overwhelming discomfort and fear. Unlike relatively brief anxious feelings, anxiety disorders are chronic, often relentless, and can worsen unless treated.

Around 10 per cent of the population has some form of anxiety disorder and around 1 per cent experience panic attacks (although twice as many women as men report them). Common among such anxiety disorders, *panic attacks* are experienced as feelings of terror that can strike suddenly with no warning. Panic attacks are so frightening that sufferers live in fear of the next one, which makes their lives a misery.

So how do you know whether you're suffering such a disorder? During a panic attack, you're likely to sweat, to experience a pounding heart, and feel faint or dizzy. These signs are often accompanied by feelings of nausea, shortness of breath, or chest pains. You may have a sense of impending doom or believe you're having a heart attack. In the midst of a panic attack, feeling that you're going to die is common.

Panic attacks are readily treatable but, left untreated, can become disabling. Sufferers tend to avoid situations where they fear an attack may strike, such as swimming, driving, using a lift, being in a confined space, and so on. About a third of sufferers' lives are so restricted that they can become housebound.

Although the chances of it are only 1 in 10, seeking medical advice is important if you feel you may suffer from any form of anxiety disorder.

Driving Safely in the Fast Lane

So you've made up your mind to become proactive and more open to new challenges. You've done the mental equivalent of 'consulting your doctor before commencing any vigorous programme of exercise'. You may be feeling a little apprehensive or even scared, but underneath that you're also feeling more alive and confident in yourself. A wellspring of joy is evident that can become your motivation to stretch yourself. Congratulations: you're growing again.

Creating a haven for yourself

You're surrounded by a whole personal development industry that offers you tools for development, many of which are right here in this book. One of the most useful tools, at this early stage of your journey, is to create a haven for yourself where the things that trigger the appropriate neurological and physiological responses in you can calm and nourish you.

If you see life as a great expedition, as peaks to be conquered, then this haven can become your growth base camp. Just as climbers establish a base camp that contains everything they need to sustain them as they make their ascents on the peaks, so you need a place for rest and recuperation (R&R) – a place you can rely on to restore you quickly and efficiently to your normal, well-balanced condition.

The key attributes your haven needs to provide are:

✔ A means of restoring your physical state from agitated to restful and alert.

✔ A means of restoring your spirits from careworn to inspired.

✔ A means of restoring your energy from depleted to abundant.

Restoring your body, mind, and spririt efficiently is possible through a combination of physical rest and relaxation, focus, and routine. Your objective is to create a system that delivers to you the three attributes in the preceding list in 30 minutes or so.

Creating your haven may be easier to do than to describe, so follow these simple steps. Later, when you get the hang of it, you can vary it to suit yourself, but keep it consistent each time you do it, as the habitual element of doing it the same way every time is an important part of the process.

1. **Go to a quiet corner in your room, your home, park, or garden where you can sit comfortably and be undisturbed for 20 to 30 minutes.**

   Just sitting quietly in this place allows your body and mind to quieten, which can do a lot to restore you when you're feeling a bit frazzled by events. The more you use your haven, the more powerful this immediate calming becomes as your mind and body anticipate the rest that is to come.

2. **Relax and breathe gently with awareness for 4 to 5 minutes.**

   Breathing is an important aspect of your mind/body coordination, and you can use it to create any effect you want. Right now you want to be relaxed and centred.

   When you're stressed or anxious, you breathe shallowly. This change happens naturally but can take quite a long time to get back to normal; meanwhile, you continue to feel the effects of the physical conditions that shallow breathing creates in your body.

   To change your breathing instantly, you merely have to take it under conscious control, and the traditional way of doing so is to count monkeys!

i. Exhale all your breath.

ii. Breathe in again to the count of four monkeys (one monkey, two monkeys, three monkeys, four monkeys).

iii. Hold your breath for four monkeys.

iv. Exhale for four monkeys.

v. Finally, hold your breath with your lungs empty for four monkeys.

If this final step makes you feel dizzy, reduce the count to two monkeys until you become more used to the exercise and can comfortably hold for the four-monkey count.

You may find this conscious way of breathing odd at first and it may seem uncomfortable and artificial, but stick to it. Breathing in this way settles you down as your body eliminates the neurochemical residues that keep you excited.

You need only do monkey breathing for five minutes, but come back to the monkeys if, at any stage in the process, you begin to revisit the scenes that cause you anxiety and you feel yourself getting tight again.

3. **Do 20 minutes of visualisation.**

In *visualisation,* you engage your visual creative imagination by imagining yourself on a seashore, in a mountain meadow, or in any other idyllic place of your choosing with a gentle breeze, warming sun, and a sweet place to rest your head.

Be creative and engage all your senses in planning how you can do this visualisation:

• You can use gentle, instrumental music or natural sound recordings such as waves on a shore or rainfall. (This time *isn't* right for heavy metal music, emotionally loaded words, or anything else that's likely to create excitation in your nervous system.)

• You can simultaneously use aromatherapy oils or scented candles to engage your sense of smell. Using the same scent during visits to your haven helps create a powerful connection to your restful,

contemplative state and strengthens the habitua-
tion effect, which helps to make your haven totally
reliable in giving you the R&R you need.

- If you have a relaxation tape, this is the perfect
  place to play it. You can write your own script
  and record it so that it perfectly suits your imagi-
  native haven.

During this visualisation phase, focus on relaxing your
mind, body, and spirit. The calm, untroubled environment you cultivate here is what makes your haven so
valuable.

4. **Start taking your leave.**

   When the time comes to end your session, take a few
   minutes to return to the real world gradually. When
   your body is in this restful state, your brain waves
   switch to a slower rhythm. This rhythm provides a
   lot of the R&R effect and is the perfect antidote to
   the stress of the day. Coming out of the visualisation,
   allow your brain a few minutes to build up to the
   faster rhythm of your normal waking state.

   Switch off your music, take a few deep breaths and
   stretch; then sit quietly and contemplate for a few
   moments your experience in your haven. If you had a
   particularly pleasant visualisation, you may want to
   jot down any new elements in a special notebook so
   that you can re-visit them another time. If you think
   you fell asleep, consider how hard you've been pushing yourself. Give yourself a moment or two and then
   say goodbye to your haven until your next visit and
   come to rejoin the mainstream.

The rule when creating a haven is that whatever works for
you is okay. Experiment with the suggestions we provide
to find a way that really delivers for you. When you find
your combination, stick with it and all these sensory stimuli
become triggers for your relaxation. When you become habituated to this routine, your haven can restore your calmness
and peace on even the most trying days.

If you take the trouble to create your haven and tailor it to your
needs, always respecting it as a revered space, you come to
love your haven, and it gives you the protection and nourish-
ment you need to maintain your busy life of accomplishment.

Desert island dream

Gerald Kingsland had an unusual long-term goal: he wanted to experience life on a real desert island. He meant to live this dream for a lengthy period, so it involved lots of preparation and the acquisition of real survival skills (hunting, fishing, building shelter, and so on).

Because few people had ever done this and survived, he knew he would be properly prepared only to the extent that he had thought through everything he would have to do and taken steps to ensure that he could provide all he would need (he even advertised in the newspapers for a Girl Friday and acquired Lucy Irvine as a partner for his desert island adventure).

All of this preparation took several years, and the resulting events nearly cost the pair their lives, but they did survive and you can read their individual accounts of the story in *The Islander* by Kingsland and *Castaway: A Story of Survival* by Irvine; or see Lucy's account of it in the 1986 film, *Castaway*, with Oliver Reed and Amanda Donohoe in the roles of the castaways.

Your haven is also a good place to visualise your day ahead, your perfect sales presentation, or whatever stretch you may be facing that you want to get just right. Not just your place of safety and restoration, your haven can also become a place where the more powerful, confident versions of yourself can be born into the world in quiet perfection. The more you use it, the stronger and more dependable it becomes.

Your haven is a wonderful place for creating a vision of your future and the more detailed planning that flows from it. As you become familiar with the process and turn it into a daily routine, you can begin to develop more powerful thinking habits that will serve you for the rest of your life.

Preparing for the future

The great trick of preparing for anything is to think about what you need to achieve the perfect result rather than focusing and worrying about what may go wrong. The latter has a place in planning, but is a lot less significant than you may believe.

A powerful planning tool called the Well-Formed Outcome is an effective way of thinking about any result you want to achieve. The tool describes seven conditions that any decision or goal must satisfy in order for you maximise your chances of achieving it. You can understand these conditions most easily if you consider them as the following list of seven questions.

✔ **Is your goal something you want or something you don't want?**

In other words, are you heading *towards* an outcome that you positively want rather than running *away from* something you don't want? Knowing what you want is the most powerful first step to achieving anything.

The thinking of the 1960s generation that 'we've got to get out this place if it's the last thing we ever do' led to rejection of the austere values of the immediate post-war period. Unfortunately, it also led to many unpredicted problems, because the desire and energy for change weren't directed towards anything specific.

Few situations in life exist where you can truly say 'absolutely anything would be better than this', although you may feel that way at the time. Even your escape from a burning building will go better if you know which door leads to the fire escape. So accept and embrace your dissatisfaction with the status quo, but think through what you want instead, and state it in the positive.

✔ **Is this your goal and is its achievement within your control?**

The next thing to determine is whether the goal is really yours or whether someone else is imposing it on you. Your mother may have impressed on you the need for a good education, but her regard for learning is unlikely to get you through college unless at some point education becomes something you want for yourself.

You also need to ensure that the achievement of the goal is within your control. You may have a real desire to be loved by everyone who knows you, but such a goal isn't within your control and never can be. Your life's energy can be squandered by pursuing such a goal. On the other hand, a goal of being loving to everyone you meet *is* within your control. If this goal is your chosen outcome, a likely by-product is that many of the people you meet will be loving back to you. The key difference is that you're focused on what *you* can control.

✓ **How do you know when you're succeeding?**

In a crazy dream you may get into a game with no way of knowing whether you're winning, which is exactly what people do in real life. If your goal is to be better at your job or to become a more sympathetic spouse, how do you know that you're achieving it?

You need to set up your way of measuring success, and the clearer and more objective you can make your measure the better. In business, these measurements are often called *key performance indicators* or KPIs. The great thing about KPIs is that they're objective, clearly identified, and readily monitored. Try to do the same with your evaluation measures.

✓ **Do you know where this desire is coming from?**

To want something out of the blue is highly unusual. All your wants and desires come from somewhere inside you, and you benefit from knowing where because this knowledge may modify how you feel about them.

For example, if you want a two-seater sports car, ask yourself why. Well, it's a great car you may say, with fabulous engineering, wonderful performance, and a grand marque. The car is a status symbol that will let everyone (and you) know that you've arrived. And you've wanted one ever since your first job when you were 20.

Figuring out why you want what you want is all part of the context of your goal-setting decision. Having brought all your reasons to mind, you may decide that now you're 25, you should go for that two-seater before you're too late to enjoy it. If you're 35 though, with a wife and three children, and this car is to be your main family vehicle, you may want to modify your choice to a larger four-wheel-drive, with wonderful performance of course, providing just as great a status symbol, and more seats!

✓ **What resources do you need to achieve your goal?**

When you have your goal clearly stated, in the positive, with your KPIs clearly identified, identifying the resources you need to achieve it becomes easier. For some of your goals, you already have all the resources you need and can make a start straight off the bat. For others, though, you may not have all you need and your first steps should be to secure them.

As you continue to think about your future, your thinking naturally expands to include other people and resources that you don't have currently. That's okay. Identify what you need first, and then to come up with plans to get what you need by the time you need it.

✔ Will accomplishing this goal take away anything else that you value?

When you ask yourself what the future will look like when you achieve your dreams, also consider what will be left behind, or what will disappear. When you're rich, in your mansion at the top of the hill, you'll certainly leave today's poverty behind, but what about the positive parts of your life now: the friends, the sharing, the helping each other through difficulties. If these parts also give you things that are important to you, you need to find a way to keep them in the picture. You're far less likely to achieve your goals if they don't incorporate your core values.

✔ Does the goal identify the first step you need to take?

'Well begun is half done' goes the saying, and dreams most often become reality through action. Knowing what you need to do is imperative, and getting started is the critical first step. When you take an action, the world reacts and gives you something to work with. When you marry this action with commitment, you've an unstoppable combination.

As WH Murray, a great Scottish mountaineer, wrote (in a quote often attributed to the German poet Goethe):

Whatever you can do, or dream you can do, begin it.

Boldness has genius, power, and magic in it.

Identify your next actions constantly – and take them.

Chapter 10

Developing Your Physical Confidence

· ·

In This Chapter

▶ Noticing how your body affects your thoughts and deeds

▶ Getting more comfortable in your own skin

▶ Holding out a healthy vision of yourself

· ·

Do you jump out of bed in the morning raring to go, knowing that your physical body is in good shape, fit, healthy, and free of pain, ready to enjoy the day ahead? Or do you sluggishly grab for the first coffee, croissant, or cigarette to get you on your feet and force you into action?

When you get yourself in the best physical shape you can, you've a strong foundation for being your most confident best. Confidence takes energy, and this chapter is about getting the energy flowing for you.

Connecting Your Mind and Body

Think of your body as a car, and then realise that your body is the most complex vehicle on the planet. Some 50,000 million cells make up your body, forming your bones, muscles, nerves, skin, blood, and other organs and body tissues. None of these systems works in isolation – they all communicate through highly sophisticated pathways of information signalling.

Lark or owl?

Health guru Gillian Burn, author of *Motivation For Dummies* (Wiley), advises that your body clock relates to times of day that you feel more like doing certain things. She says: 'Our bodies have natural body rhythms and biorhythms that affect us. It's certainly true that some of us are 'larks' – at our best in the morning, waking early, and preferring to start early in the day. Other people struggle in the mornings, are happier in the afternoon and evening, and work well late into the night. These people are the 'owls'.

'In terms of confidence, a useful starting point is to understand your personal body clock and whether you're more like a lark or an owl. Then you can choose the best time of day to perform certain tasks or projects. Don't fight your body; listen and go with it.'

As you consider your mind and body as one system rather than as two separate and unrelated parts, you notice how the two are inseparable. When your state of mind is calm, clear, and focused, your physical performance is likely to be at its best. Conversely, if your mind is confused and frazzled, then you're likely to be off balance physically, experiencing symptoms from clumsiness to butterflies in your stomach.

Breakthroughs by neuroscientists over the last 30 years indicate that when an emotion is triggered, your physiology shifts even though you're not consciously aware of it. This shift sends a message back to the brain affecting virtually everything the brain does. So your performance, your ability to act with confidence, is inextricably linked with your physiology.

Many mantras, prayers, yoga, and spiritual practices can have a beneficial effect on wellbeing. By practising disciplines such as yoga, meditation, Tai Chi, and martial arts, you can develop the discipline to calm your mind and centre your body for effective action.

Brain boosting the biceps

Just as physical exercise can boost the brain, researchers have found that how you think can boost the body. The *New Scientist* reported on a study in 2001 at the Cleveland Clinic Foundation in Ohio. Researchers got volunteers to spend just 15 minutes a day simply thinking about exercising their biceps. After 12 weeks, their arms were 13 per cent stronger. And all this added strength happened without any physical training.

 One of the quickest ways to get your physiology regulated is through changing your breathing patterns. Practise simple deep breathing exercises every day and focus your energy on your heart as you do so. When you find yourself in a situation of tension, breathe through the situation rather than reacting with anger or negative emotion. Breathing helps you conserve your reserves of energy. (Chapters 9 and 11 introduce you to our monkey breathing steps – an easy calming technique.)

Considering What Makes You Healthy

What does healthy mean to you? Perhaps your measure relates to the food you eat, the exercise you take, whether you floss your teeth each day, or the medical treatment you receive. Take a moment to write down what makes you feel healthy.

In the Western world today, a rising tide of people is becoming chronically obese, which in the longer term produces severe health problems, including heart disease and Type 2 diabetes. Regular exercise combined with a healthy diet is essential if you want to live to a healthy old age. And feeling healthy makes a huge difference to your overall confidence.

 If you're struggling to increase your exercise, cultivate an exercise buddy to walk or run with you or join you in a sport regularly. Kate has been playing tennis with friends each week for many years, turning the game into a social occasion that is friendly and fun as well as healthy.

Health and fitness are not the same. You can be superfit, yet damage your wellbeing from over-exercising or poor eating habits.

Releasing stress, staying healthy

Stress is a key factor in modern living and working as your time, money, and energy feels the squeeze. Financial pressures plus family issues such as divorce or caring for young children and elders take their toll at home. Increasingly, in tough economic times modern workers are experiencing substantial job insecurity, longer working hours, increased travel, and lowered morale. Workplace stress also damages health, happiness, and home relationships. All of these things can have detrimental effects on your self-confidence.

Stress is not all bad – it can create excitement, innovation, and motivation. Yet when it crosses the dividing line from a positive stretch to a negative pressure, you feel out of control. An excess of stress leads to hypertension and greatly increases your risk of heart disease.

You may think of stress and depression as strictly psychological problems, but they've an effect on the whole body, not just the quality of your mental processes. You suffer physically as you become more gloomy and pessimistic. Your confidence and physiology are so closely linked. That's why managing your stress levels is so important.

Normal everyday stress affects your body and can:

- ✔ Raise your blood pressure.
- ✔ Make your heart beat faster.
- ✔ Restrict the flow of blood to the skin.
- ✔ Deplete your immune system and resistance to infection.
- ✔ Disrupt the digestive processes.
- ✔ Create a feeling of edginess inside.

Stress can become extreme as a number of work and domestic issues get compounded. This situation happens, for example, if you're working long hours for a period of time and can't see the end to it, then you suffer the death or ill health of a loved one, face financial difficulties, or your marriage breaks down.

Your body is pre-programmed with a basic 'fight or flight' response to keep you safe. This program may show itself as flight, as when you physically can't get out of bed to go to work or you experience panic attacks – or fight, when you lose your temper or lash out at someone unexpectedly.

Getting stress out of your system

Getting negative stress out of your system involves building good everyday habits. By this statement, we mean regular practices that keep your system functioning smoothly.

Don't wait until you feel bad. Instead, make sure that you develop stress-relieving habits while all is well so that you're better prepared when your immune system is most vulnerable.

Delegates on Kate's workshops based around her book *Live Life. Love Work* (Capstone Books) create their own set of everyday habits to stay centred and quieten the mind. These habits range from physical postures such as the Yoga sun salutation – a range of movements to stretch and energise the body – through to problem-solving strategies and mentally creating a quiet place that they can visit in their heads to feel calm.

Talking things over with a coach or mentor can help give you a better perspective on the issues underlying your stress. You need to objectively identify the root causes for the tension and work on these causes in order to move on happily. Joining a support group of people in a similar situation is also helpful – whether this group is a group of mums of toddlers or a job-search group.

Raising the feel-good factors

Think about what gives you the feel-good factor. In Figure 10-1 is space for you to evaluate the positives in your life from various angles. Then when you're feeling down, you can spend a minute circling round each spoke of the wheel inhaling the good vibes. This activity unlocks the endorphins in your body that boost your immune system and help you to feel better about yourself.

What is your real age?

At www.realage.com, you can measure how fast your body is aging. The idea is that whereas your calendar age simply reflects the number of birthdays you've had, RealAge gauges the physiological age of your body and measures your rate of aging.

Certain health choices can slow and even reverse the rate of aging. In highly stressful times, your RealAge can be as much as 32 years older than your calendar age. Laughter, mental activity, and vitamins are just three of 44 factors that promote age reduction. And the good news is that even choices made late in life make a difference. People who start exercising in their fifties and sixties, or even later, show considerable health benefits.

For each section of the wheel, capture two or three positive suggestions. These suggestions may trigger a memory of an event or place that made your feel good or a reminder of something to do like playing a piece of music, looking at a favourite picture or object. The categories are:

- ✔ **Places** you've visited or would like to see – these places can include cities, beaches, mountains, gardens, galleries, or buildings.
- ✔ **People and animals** can be those you know and others you don't but who inspire or interest you.
- ✔ **Exercises** include your favourite sports as well as mental exercises.
- ✔ **Objects** are things of beauty; items that trigger a happy memory.
- ✔ **Events** such as holidays, anniversaries, and celebrations – important times in your life.
- ✔ **Pictures and symbols** may be items of art, postcards, icons, and photographs.
- ✔ **Smells and tastes** are your favourite food and aromas.
- ✔ **Words and sounds** include music, poems, mantras, and affirmations.

Make a note of these suggestions in each sector of the wheel shown in Figure 10-1 as a reminder to give you a boost when you need it.

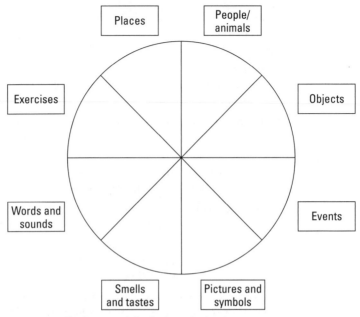

Places

People/ animals

Exercises

Objects

Words and sounds

Events

Smells and tastes

Pictures and symbols

Figure 10-1: Circling round the feel-good wheel.

Following the golden rules for a healthy diet

You wouldn't consider putting the wrong kind of fuel in your car, so why do it to your body? What you eat and how much water you drink has a major impact on your energy and thus your confidence. So eat well and with awareness.

Put the brakes on your eating at moments when feeling stressed, anxious, or over-excited, because losing awareness of what is going in your body, how hungry you feel, and what the best food is for you right now is all too easy during those times. Instead of grabbing fast food on the run, step back, choose the more healthy option, and get ready to savour every mouthful.

Here are some more healthy diet tips:

✔ **Drink water:** Unless you want to end up as a dried-out prune, drink 1½ to 2 litres of pure, clean water every day. Your body naturally loses several litres of fluid each day. Water is critical to help you cleanse your body, eliminating waste and toxins. Often when you think that you're hungry, you're actually thirsty.

✔ **Examine your oils:** Avoid chemicals and additives in the fats and oils you choose. Hemp seed oil is one of the richest sources of essential fatty acids omega-3 and omega-6.

✔ **Choose brown, not white:** Brown rice is more cleansing for your immune system, and go for wholemeal breads and pastas every time.

✔ **Snack on seeds:** The zinc in pumpkin and sunflower seeds boosts your energy. Seeds are instant and tasty.

✔ **Don't add salt:** Save the salt for when you swim in the sea. Cut back on salt and look after your blood pressure.

✔ **Go with greens:** Eat leafy greens every day. Watercress, spinach, cabbage, lettuce, Swiss chard, mint, and parsley are rich in minerals and vitamins.

✔ **Avoid tobacco:** Get away from all forms of smoking. Whether the smoke is yours or someone else's, smoking depletes the nutrients in your body.

✔ **Re-educate your sweet tooth:** Eating regularly and well keeps your blood sugar stable and save the need for a sugar fix. As well as cutting down on sweets, biscuits, and cakes, beware the hidden sugar in processed food such as flavoured yoghurt, fruit and carbonated drinks, and sauces.

If you're good at keeping to the healthy rules 80 per cent of the time, you're well on your way to making a healthy diet a natural way of eating.

Believing in your health

Beliefs are the working principles on which you act. They're not proven facts but working assumptions. To develop your physical confidence, believing that looking after your well-being to the best of your ability is both possible and desirable is helpful.

The following belief statements can support you. Try them on for size by taking one principle a day and acting from that position.

✔ When I'm healthy my confidence levels rise.

✔ I can create a healthy life for myself.

✔ It's never too late to start being healthy.

✔ I have a strong appetite for physical exercise.

✔ I can look after my health in many different ways.

✔ My health is my responsibility.

✔ I can accept an injury or illness and still be a healthy person.

✔ I can discover new things from a number of role models.

✔ Fun and laughter play a great part in my wellbeing.

✔ Keeping moving is important.

✔ My vitality and wellbeing are infectious.

Looking Forward to Your Healthy Future Self

Your behaviour today has a direct impact on your health in the future. Your health is one area of your life that you can't afford to ignore.

Sports coaches often film you playing your sport and then compare your movements, shots, strokes, or swings with a sporting hero. If you had a video camera, what picture would you record of your own physical wellbeing right now? Now fast forward that image and see what you look like one year, five years, and ten years from now, and at the end of your life. Imagine the image you're going to see if you carry on as you're doing just now and feel how that affects your confidence. What, if any, changes do you want to make?

To be healthy and energetic, you need fuel from good-quality food and water, adequate rest, a healthy environment, sufficient exercise, variety and challenge in your work and play, and supportive people around you.

Chapter 11

Raising Your Voice

*P*ublic speaking to a group or large audience, and even regular speaking in a business meeting, can feel highly artificial. If you've ever sat through a dull committee meeting you may have mused that too many people like the sound of their own voice. Yet actually, for every one of those people there are a dozen who hate to hear themselves speak or else don't believe they've anything worthwhile to say. To become more powerful in the world, you need to feel able to speak up authentically in all situations.

To say that your voice is one of your most important links to the rest of humanity is a truism, but have you ever really stopped to think about the fundamental importance of your voice, and how debilitating it can be to your life if your 'voice' in the world is less than powerful?

A powerful voice in this context doesn't mean the power to fill an auditorium with sound, like a Shakespearian actor. It means giving authentic voice to the real you as you live and breathe, and go about your work. This voice is what links you to the rest of the world.

In this chapter, you discover how you can use your voice to project the more powerful and confident version of yourself.

Speaking Out with Confidence

Why is public speaking so nerve wracking? Why, when confronted unexpectedly by their dream date or their boss, do sitcom characters become incoherent, mumbling idiots (and you laugh because you recognise yourself in the situation)? How can it be that something so natural as speaking, which you've been practising more or less continuously since you first discovered how to do it, can at times become so difficult?

Children joke about the centipede who loses his ability to walk when someone asks him how he does it; the same thing happens with speaking. When speaking becomes self-conscious, for any reason, you get caught up in its mechanics and lose your easy, natural groove.

To find your public voice and gain the confidence to speak out, you need something to say (a message) and someone to say it to (an audience). And you need something connecting you in that moment to the person or group you're speaking to, which is commonly called *rapport* – a shared view of the world within which you've room for disagreement. To achieve all this, you need to deal with anything standing in the way.

Listening to yourself

Have you ever heard yourself speak on tape? Did you find it a shocking experience to hear your own voice 'from the outside'? It sounds so different from your voice as you experience it from inside your head that you may assume the recording quality is at fault until others confirm that you sound exactly that way in real life. You may have been surprised or dismayed by the poor quality of your diction, or the strength of your accent, and have made an unconscious decision to do something about it or else never speak in public again. However, deciding not to speak in public for any reason is ridiculous and unsustainable.

Speaking with your local accent and in your regional dialect can help in building rapport. Be proud of your accent – which is part of who you are – and be prepared to work on your public speaking skills a little in line with the advice in this chapter.

The most common problems with speaking in public are clarity and diction. As your first schoolteacher probably told you, if you sit up and speak clearly you will be heard – heard all over the world.

What your accent says about you

Spoken English is a language with a rich and varied heritage. In the North of England, certain dialect words have remained unchanged since mediaeval times. Off the coast of North Carolina in the USA, the speech of isolated communities still closely resembles that of the west countrymen who left England to settle there in the 17th century.

Received pronunciation (RP) is one particular accent of British English based on the speech of the middle classes of southeast England. Characteristic of the accent used at the public schools and Oxford and Cambridge Universities, RP was the accent adopted by the British Broadcasting Corporation (BBC) at the advent of public broadcasting, and after the Second World War, RP became the national standard of the educated English.

Today, this domination of broadcasting by the RP accent has been rightly consigned to history. Now the upper and educated classes are just as likely to try to cover up their posh accents as vice versa. A new egalitarian accent, Estuary English, has been born. Today's Britain is at last becoming more interested in what is being said rather than the accent in which it is being said.

Practising to avert disaster

When Oliver faced the daunting prospect of making the best man's speech at a large wedding, he turned to his father for help. His dad was an experienced public speaker and consulting him seemed natural as it was his wedding and Oliver was only 13 years old.

Dad gave him permission to tell a few jokes in the tradition of the best man's speech and over a couple of weeks they worked out an entertaining speech that would take 8–10 minutes to deliver. Oliver typed it into the computer. With three weeks to go to the wedding, he was ready with time to spare.

Oliver was still nervous, yet felt much better now that he knew what he was going to say. Then Dad delivered his bombshell: he wasn't going to allow Oliver to read his speech from the prepared paper. Instead, Dad recommended that he read it out loud in his bedroom 12 times before the day, then prepare five or six bullet points to act as his only memory aides.

Oliver probably read his speech more like 20 times over the next two weeks. Then, the week before the big day, his Dad helped him to pull out five bullet points that would help him to remember the key structure so he could speak in a natural way when he came to give the speech. He practised in his bedroom and although it was a bit shorter, at six minutes, he found he was able to do it.

Then on the day, disaster! As the company sat down to eat, with the speeches the next item on the wedding agenda, Oliver's wedding nightmare came true: he had misplaced his bullet points, and had no time now to think about them, or ask his dad who wasn't even sitting next to him. He was scared witless.

When it was his turn he stood up to speak, took a deep breath, and started – but nothing came out. He started again, his mouth moved, but no sound came out. It was now or never. He took a small sip of water and, with the audience literally on the edge of their seats, he began, a little hesitantly at first but soon gaining momentum.

He found he could remember the bullets, and even whole sentences. As he went along the words came, and when he realised he had missed out a piece of information he needed for a joke he went back to it, quite naturally, as he would have in a conversation. His audience of family, friends, and relatives laughed at the jokes and were spellbound. Oliver felt a binding rapport with them as he told his stories.

At the end, the applause and shouting were amazing. He seemed to have been on his feet for only a couple of minutes but the wedding video, which captured every nuance and detail, confirms that it was 10 minutes exactly. He stole the show, and there was nobody more pleased than his dad, who even had a tear in his eye. Would he do it again? Yes, definitely – although not for a while!

Breathing to improve your speaking

Shallow breathing is a common problem when you're faced with any kind of public speaking.

Rapid, shallow breathing can reduce the level of carbon dioxide in your blood, which reduces the flow of blood through your body. Then, even though your lungs are taking in all the oxygen your body should need, your brain and body experience a shortage. This shortage can leave you feeling tense, nervous, and unable to think clearly.

The solution, which is well known to singers and those who play wind instruments, is to breathe deeply from the diaphragm or abdomen. If, like most people, you've little idea how to do this, read on.

Feeling how you breathe

First, locate your diaphragm: place your right hand flat on your stomach just above your navel and below the bottom of your rib cage. Now, take a series of short sniffs as though you're trying to detect the smell of something on fire. You should feel the area under your hand moving in and out. This is your diaphragm. Now, place your left hand on your upper chest just below your collarbone, keeping your right hand over your diaphragm. Take a few normal breaths.

If you're breathing correctly, you feel the rhythmic rising and falling movement of your breathing in your right hand. If you feel movement under your left hand, you're breathing from your chest – not what you want.

Discovering how to breathe through your diaphragm

Breathing through your diaphragm gives you the powerful voice you want. Follow these steps:

1. **Place your right hand over your diaphragm and your left hand on your chest.**

2. **Purse your lips as though you're about to whistle, and breathe out slowly to a count of five monkeys (count one monkey, two monkeys, and so on to yourself) while tightening your stomach muscles.**

(Chapter 9 has a complete explanation of monkey breathing.)

3. **Breathe in slowly through your nose to a count of three monkeys.**

   Feel your right hand rising with the diaphragm.

4. **Pause slightly for two monkeys and then breathe out again to a count of five as in Step 2.**

If you practise this technique for just a few minutes before every meal and again at odd times throughout the day, you soon become habituated to this more effective way of breathing. As soon as you get your muscles trained, your diaphragm can do 80 per cent of the incessant work of your breathing for the rest of your life. Proper breathing gives you the platform you need for a powerful voice.

When you're comfortable with diaphragmatic breathing, you can add in another two steps to improve your voice quality further:

✔ In Step 2, instead of pursing your lips, add in a gentle 'Ah' sound for the full exhalation stage. Keep this 'Ah' going until you run out of air.

✔ When you have the rhythm going, drop both your hands to your sides and bounce your shoulders gently but rapidly up and down as you breathe out to 'Ah'. Doing so releases tension from your vocal cords and helps to prepare your voice for speaking.

Now your voice is ready, what are you going to say?

Saying What You Mean and Meaning What You Say

A good rule for effective communication is always to say what you mean and mean what you say. This rule isn't an excuse to be rude or haughty, but is a solid basis from which you can come to know your truth and speak it out. Following this rule is good for your integrity and quickly cements your reputation as a communicator of real power and persuasion.

Holding onto your integrity

What does it mean to you to have integrity? Perhaps you immediately think of things like keeping your word and not telling lies or otherwise being dishonest. Integrity does mean these things, and more besides, and is an essential element of the most powerful, confident you.

Think of your integrity as your inner sense of wholeness, coming from a consistent sense of who you are being in all parts of your world. When you do anything with integrity, you're being authentic; you're acting or speaking without pretence, *not even to yourself*. Having integrity is critical to your power and congruence in the world, and is at the heart of your confidence to take action.

Sadly, your personal integrity and authenticity can be too easily sacrificed on the altar of rubbing along with your friends and neighbours or looking good to the boss. This rubbing along can be a massive own goal in your game of life that can cost you far more than you bargained for. A white lie over here, a little 'talking up' over there, and pretty soon you won't know who you are or what you really stand for.

The single most powerful step you can take to improve your confidence and power in the world is to restore your integrity.

Table 11-1 contains an integrity checklist. Each time you violate any item on the list, you leak personal power and confidence. Each time you honour an item, you become more powerful in the world and build your reserves of confidence.

Before you start your personal evaluation, draw a mental line under everything you have ever done in your life, good or bad, until this moment. Wipe your slate clean. Your new integrity account is now open for business.

Table 11-1	Integrity Checklist
Actions that Increase Your Personal Power and Confidence	*Actions that Reduce Your Personal Power and Confidence*
Honouring your word and keeping your promises.	Failing to back up your words with actions.
Being honest with yourself and with others.	Acting or speaking in a way that causes real harm to others.
Accepting people as they are and judging only their actions.	Acting as superior to others or browbeating someone weaker than yourself.
Treating others with respect and candour.	Failing to act in the right way because no one is watching.
Letting people know where you stand on important issues.	Not giving of your best.
Being genuine and transparent with people. Not deceiving through silence or inaction.	Not following your conscience.
Being true to your values and purpose.	Not practising what you preach.
Living up to your standards and doing the right thing.	Manipulating or misleading others (or yourself).
Admitting and accepting your own mistakes.	Telling white lies to look good or to avoid looking bad.
Saying what you mean and meaning what you say.	Using bluff or bluster to get your own way.
Walking your talk.	Pretending to be anything other than your authentic self.

Having difficult conversations

So, you've opened your new integrity account and are determined to take only those actions that increase your power and confidence. Then your wife comes into the room wearing a new outfit that makes her look dumpy and sad. 'How do I look?' she asks (at this point you mentally run down a few relevant items on your list: being honest, saying what you mean, treating others with respect, not speaking in a way that causes harm to others). What do you do?

Only you know the honest answer to this. The scenario is a set-up, of course, and deliberately difficult. It would have been a lot better all round to share your new insights and intentions with your partner before she asked you the fateful question. But the harsh truth you may discover here is that the communication in many of your relationships lacks integrity, and that damages the relationship more than you may realise.

At some level, your wife knows that she doesn't look good in the outfit. She may even have known that in the shop but felt obliged to follow through with the assistant who was lying through her teeth in order to make the sale. If so, your wife is really asking you to make the situation okay. If you say she looks good and leave it at that, you're cheating her just like the sales assistant did. When she wears the outfit to a function and hates the way she looks in it, where does that leave you?

So, before this scenario can happen, a better move is to have *authenticity conversations* with your family, friends, and work colleagues, during which you tell them that you're focusing on how to be more confident and powerful in the world and what this means about saying what you mean and meaning what you say. Ask them to help you by being honest with you and keeping you true to your word. You may be surprised how your public repositioning in this way changes the dynamics of your relationships and gives them much more integrity.

If you really want to take on the full restoration of your integrity, you can go back to friends and colleagues from your past where relationships suffered through lack of integrity on your part and acknowledge it. Don't get into the blame game, even if the other person wants to. A simple acknowledgement will do: 'I just want you to know that I enjoyed most of our time together and, even though it ended badly, those good times were important to me.' Try this acknowledgement and you'll be amazed by how it makes you feel. You can stand taller and be more present in the world directly as a result.

Recognising that the Message Is More than Words

A well-known fact on the professional speaking circuit is that the words the speaker uses are responsible for only 7 per cent of the impact of the communication. Voice and delivery add a further 38 per cent and body posture and movement add the rest – an amazing 55 per cent. So although word and voice are critical (without them communication does not exist), bringing your body into play adds massively to your impact.

Even though many speakers know the facts, they often fail dismally to do anything with them and remain stuck behind the podium or, worse, begin to strut around the stage and wave their hands, generally getting in their own way and detracting from the impact of the message.

In the following sections, you find ways to present your message in a congruent fashion.

Visiting the natural school

Two schools of thought exist on body language: the theatrical school and the natural school. You're already an expert natural communicator as you have been practising it for so long you've achieved unconscious competence. So, when you're excited you gesture, when you're intense you point and fix your subject with your eyes, when you're playful you throw back your head and raise your eyes to the sky.

Problems arise only when you become self-conscious or uncomfortable. A tight-fitting shirt at an interview can do this to you, or an audience that looks blank or hostile. Sometimes you become intimidated simply by the size or seniority of your audience. Whatever the cause, the minute you lose your natural groove, you can begin to struggle. You're not sure what to do with your hands, you jiggle the coins in your pocket, you stand in front of your visuals, and you generally feel and act like a clown.

Acting out the theatrical school

The theatrical school, the other hand, has little confidence in your ability to communicate with natural power to an audience and so advocates tried and tested gestures that you acquire like drills until they become hard-wired. The problem with this approach is that speakers often betray their drilling and never look natural or comfortable. This can set the audience on edge and detract from the power of the message.

Finding your authentic approach

The best solution is usually the most authentic, and the authentic you is the one to develop. Rather than memorise a performance on stage, discover how to be yourself even when you're under pressure.

The techniques for authenticity aren't so different from one-to-one communication. As you gain in confidence and power from your increased understanding of who you are and what you want, you'll be able to influence groups quite naturally.

Look at the people you're speaking to, be prepared to let them see how you feel about your message, be attentive and curious as to how they receive it. If you proceed in this way, you're much more likely deliver a powerful, natural performance.

Like most other things in life, if you've good technique, you can improve your public speaking with practise. Speaking clubs such as Toastmasters International provide a supportive environment in which you've the opportunity to develop communication and leadership skills, which in turn foster self-confidence and personal growth. Check them out at www. toastmasters.org.

Chapter 12

Getting the Result You Want

. . . .

In This Chapter

▶ Planning to achieve your biggest goals ever

▶ Identifying the source of your fear and tackling it

▶ Working out what you really, really want to achieve

▶ Ensuring that your 'why' is always bigger than your 'what'

▶ Adopting the Guaranteed Success Formula to deliver your dreams

. . . .

*T*hink about something you'd *really, really* like to do or the kind of person you want to become. No matter how big your imagination, this chapter enables you to prepare your strategy and move forward. This chapter helps you boost your confidence, give yourself the extra power to take action, and follow through to ultimate success.

In this chapter we help you let go of fear that's holding you back, define a target you want to work towards, boost your motivation, and think about the implications of achieving your dream. And finally, we apply the Guaranteed Success Formula that we introduce in Chapter 3 to help you to work in detail on your dream without the possibility of failure.

Shaking Off Fear

Your fear of failure, of crashing in a heap at your first attempt and looking bad in front of others, is likely to be the highest hurdle in getting what you want. Anything else you tell yourself is probably an attempt to divert your attention from this simple fact: you're scared to take the action you need to take to get the result you want. Before you can move onto getting what you want, you need to let go of the fear that blocks you.

Understanding your physiological response

Your mental and physical states (or *physiology*) are inextricably linked. Fear often shows up in the body as a sick feeling in the stomach or restricted movement in the neck. Fear is an emotion, and the biological basis of your fear is an ancient fundamental response – the *fight or flight* response. When confronted by threat, you need instant energy, to fight your way free or to run away. So, when you're in a scary situation, adrenalin surges through your body, your heart rate and blood pressure rise, you sweat, and you feel agitated, ready to explode into action.

In today's modern and relatively secure world, this response is still great if you need to escape from a mugger or dive into water to rescue a child. But you don't need the response in many of the more common situations that scare you. Too often the 'fight or flight' response floods your body with chemicals and leaves you in a worse state than before.

Managing fear by observing earlier breakthroughs

Managing self-defeating biological responses (see the previous section) to challenges in your life is the key that unlocks the most confident version of yourself. You can't change your biology, but you can manage it better and build a life that's healthier for both your mind and your body.

One powerful shortcut to confidence shows up when you reproduce your own most powerful thinking from the times when you've already been successful. Another is to gain knowledge from strong characters in history and other role models.

Remembering your own successes

Try this exercise to recall times when you felt confident and achieved what you wanted.

1. **Think back to a time when you felt really confident about something and you pulled it off.**

   Choose anything at all: when you made the perfect golf drive, passed your driving test, gave a party, ran a 10-kilometre race, spoke at a wedding, passed an important test or interview or took to the dance floor. Pick a specific event where you were confident that you would get a good result and you did.

2. **Remember how you felt before.**

   How did things look, sound, and feel? Maybe you had butterflies in your tummy, or your hands were shaking a little. Deep down you knew you could pull it off, yet you experienced a little frisson of thrill at your risk taking. Hold that sensation.

3. **Consider the next confidence tester that's coming up for you.**

   You may think of an exam, date, or sporting fixture where you want to succeed.

4. **Imagine stepping into that future situation, bringing with you the memory and sensations of your earlier success.**

   Savour the knowledge that you've all the resources you need to succeed. Based on your earlier confident experiences, you already know that confidence isn't about knowing exactly how you'll do something; it isn't about being certain that you'll be successful first time, every time. Confidence is the recognition that you can figure out the way to get it done if you care enough about the result and apply what you do know.

Following your hero

Begin by finding the best example you can find of somebody who took heroic action that led to a successful result. For example, delve back into history to the tale of Hannibal crossing the Alps to attack Rome with his elephants. Or consider an inventor like Edison with his famous 10,000 attempts to invent the light-bulb, or great artists taking on massive projects, or

Olympic sportsmen and women breaking world records. Find any hero who appeals to you – the bigger and more audacious the hero's exploits, the better for the purposes of this exercise.

When you've a good example in your mind, work your way through the following four steps:

1. **Describe your hero's action in a couple of clear sentences.**

   For example, Hannibal was a Carthaginian military commander resisting Roman expansion into North Africa. His only chance of victory was to surprise the Romans by crossing the Alps from Spain, in winter, to attack them in their own backyard with his war elephants. This was one of the most audacious military strategies in history, something that the Romans considered impossible.

2. **Consider why your hero wanted to achieve this objective.**

   Hannibal had been raised by his father, also a military commander, to resist the hated Romans in their expansion into Africa. The greatness of Carthage and the mercantile civilisation of North Africa were at dire risk. Hannibal knew that his elephant cavalry would make the Romans panic and that by attacking Rome he would force their military into peace talks.

3. **Consider why your hero believed that she (or he) would come up with a solution.**

   Morale was high and Hannibal believed that his men would beat the Romans if their backs were against the wall. Hannibal didn't care how they did it, but all their lives depended upon finding a route through with their elephants.

4. **Consider whether your hero used some version of the Guaranteed Success Formula ('I don't know the way, but I'll find it') to achieve the objective.**

   Hannibal is attributed as saying: 'We will find a way, or make one!' If one way didn't work, he would just keep on going until another way was found or created.

Invincible self-belief and ultimate confidence is the Guaranteed Success Formula in action. It's simply about taking action even when you don't yet know the right way to succeed.

The good news is that you don't have to be taking elephants across a mountain range to engage exactly the same thinking as Hannibal to achieve what you want in life. With that as your assurance, why wouldn't you be confident in whatever you set out to achieve?

Naming and Focusing on Your Target for Confident Action

Think about what you want, and where this achievement is going to take you. What is it that you yearn for? What changes do you dream of? Chapter 2 gives you lots of tools and tips for exploring where you may have been holding back.

So what are your dreams? Are they worthy of you, or do you perhaps hold back through fear or conditioning from well-meaning parents, teachers, and friends? The bigger your dreams, the more they impact the world beyond your own needs and desires, and the more strength, energy, and power you can tap into in pursuit of them. No dream is too big.

What goal will you pick to follow through on until you're successful? Choose something meaningful to you, such as a new career or way of working, a new relationship or home move, or perhaps something a little more specific like completing a photography course or climbing a mountain in Africa for charity.

At the highest level, if you're clear on your chosen life's purpose, you may find yourself dreaming an extraordinary dream that nobody else has; a dream that keeps you pumped up and fully engaged for the rest of your life. But most people aren't aspiring to this level. Most people just know that their life would be enriched by a bigger job or a loving relationship or respite from their fear of flying.

Visualising that you achieve your goal

Whatever you choose to work on, you increase your chances of following through with the action if you've a clear picture of yourself succeeding.

In Chapter 9 we show you how to create a haven for meditation, reflection, and thinking. No need for an elaborate physical space, any quiet corner will do, but you make meditating a habit if you keep to a special place and introduce consistent elements of ritual into the time you spend there. Think of this as your dream corner. If you don't have one yet, take any quiet time and space and let your imagination take flight.

See yourself with the result you want, allowing the image to develop. Enjoy the scene unfolding in front of you in full colour, as in a movie. Let the scene be vivid, in all its vibrancy. See the success you're achieving. Hear the sounds and conversations taking place. If you're speaking, listen to the words you're saying, and the tone and manner in which you're speaking. If others are speaking, listen to their words. Hear any other sounds, like sounds of excitement or music, or notice the silence. Allow yourself to feel what you feel like in your body when you succeed. Notice any pleasant tastes and smells and savour each and every one of them.

Stay in your imaginary vision as long as you can, and when you feel your attention waning, take yourself from the scene and move it into the distance, letting it fade as it disappears. Congratulations, you've just given yourself a new life experience. Read on to discover how to use it in the journey towards your goal.

Turning the dream into reality

Your unconscious mind can't tell the difference between what you vividly imagine and the same event really happening. If you complete the exercise in the previous section and visualise that you achieve your goal, your unconscious mind now thinks that you've already achieved your objective before. It knows what this success looks, sounds and feels like, and it knows how to go about achieving the same or an even better result next time. All you have to do is to put into action the things you imagined.

Do you know anyone who's so reliable that when she takes on an obligation you know that she'll get the job done, no matter what? People like this are valuable in organisations. If you're a manager and you delegate a task to someone like this, you know that you can stop worrying, or forget about the task because that task is as good as done.

This is the level of commitment you now need to bring to realising your vision of success. All you have to do is mark out the steps and take the required action using the Guaranteed Success Formula.

Making Your 'Why' Bigger

Why do you want to achieve your goal? Friedrich Nietzsche said that people can deal with almost any adversity in life provided they've a big enough desire to deal with it. What drives you forward isn't the things you want to achieve, but the reasons you want to achieve them.

It's not the *what* but the *why* that carries you through the trials of life to your ultimate success. Provided your why is big enough, you eventually succeed because you won't give up until you do.

So *why* do you want to achieve the result you're after? You've a reason, of course, but how big and strong is it? If your dream is just a mild fancy, a 'nice to have', then you're likely to quit at the first setback. But if your dream is an absolute *must have* – for example, the life of a child depends upon your achieving the result – then you're unlikely to give up ever, no matter what stands in your way. The following sections help you think about your motivation.

Considering what achieving the goal means

How much do you want your result? Think of everything that achieving this result will do for you. You'll get the immediate gratification, of course, but are there important secondary benefits? Will this success be a life first for you? Will it open the door to other opportunities? To further successes? If you can achieve this result, what other results could you achieve? What will others think of you? If you're changing others' opinions or perceptions of you, what other doors will this change open?

With these thoughts in mind, check whether your dream is big enough. Should you be raising your standards higher? Are you holding yourself back? Might a bigger goal excite you more and make it even more likely that you can follow through successfully? What are you prepared to do to win the outcome you desire? Will you go that last mile? Will you never give up, no matter what?

The more positive and pleasurable things you can link to being successful in this endeavour, the more effort you put in and the more likely you are to succeed. Many hidden benefits exist if you spend time trying to pull them out. Do that now and go on to the next section to a more powerful set of questions.

Adding up the cost of failing

On the other side of motivation is pain; in this case, the pain of not succeeding in your chosen task or, worse still, not even starting it. Failure isn't fun in any circumstances, but what would such a failure mean? Would it be unbearable and unacceptable? Normally, we don't recommend negative thinking, but here you're making a brief visit to The Dark Side to reinforce your determination and motivation to put everything into achieving the result you're after. Paint this picture of failure just as vividly as you can – quickly, go for it!

Okay, you don't get the promotion, but what exactly will failure cost you? What will it cost your family? Money? Challenge? Respect? What about your health and sense of self-worth? Even bigger than this, if you're really the man or woman for the job, what will failure cost your company? Your boss isn't infallible; what if you let her make a mistake and give the promotion to someone less able. This mistake may end up costing the jobs of your whole department or section. Think bigger. What would planet Earth lose if you don't achieve your goal? What cosmic event would no longer take place? What potential would be lost from human evolution? What part of you will die if you give up on your dream?

When you feel as excited as you can get looking at the upside of success, and as miserable as you can feel contemplating the downside of not going for your goal with enough energy, you're ready to consider the impact of achieving your dream (see the next section).

Considering the Impact of Your Dream

The motivational speaker Bob Proctor says that the achievement of your dreams is merely a by-product of the real prize, which is who you become in the process of achieving the dream.

If you've spent time identifying with the result you want (see the earlier section 'Naming and Focusing on Your Target for Confident Action') and you've motivated yourself to go for it (see the section 'Making Your 'Why' Bigger), you're now in a good position to consider the kind of person you'll become by achieving this dream. If your dream is big, it is likely to impact on you in major ways. Check that the impact is going to be mostly positive or else the dream isn't right for you.

Checking in with your values

How will your dream sit with you after you achieve it? Does the goal fit with the values you explore in Chapter 5?

For many years, Ken had a dream to own a Maserati. Initially, there was something about the romance of it. He had fallen in love with the brand name years before as a child, listening to motor-racing legend Stirling Moss talking about racing Maseratis in the international Grand Prix. As he grew up, the idea disappeared from his awareness for a couple of decades, but it reappeared at a time when he had come into money and was looking to buy a prestige car.

Ken looked at a Maserati in the showroom, taking along his 17-year-old son, who encouraged him to buy it. Ken spoke to the salesman who was, naturally, full of enthusiasm for the new range that was re-establishing the brand globally. But something about the decision was nagging at him and Ken couldn't bring himself to take the car out for the test drive.

Victims of the wrong dream

Sir Bob Geldof, who organised Live Aid and changed the world's appreciation of African famine and its causes, called his autobiography *Is That It?*. Having made it as a rock star, he found his celebrity lifestyle shallow and largely meaningless. He went on to dedicate his life to the removal of poverty and debt from Africa, changing people's appreciation of the debt burden and the effects of unfair trading practices. He's confident that he can solve the African trade problem, and is driven by this dream. He'll be remembered as one of history's great campaigners.

Geldof is exceptional. Every day, newspapers are full of stories of other celebrities who are chasing, living, and being consumed by the media dream. This dream is an externally imposed vision of success, usually dependent upon the favour of a few media tycoons who 'make and break' celebrity. TV screens are packed with reality shows, including one that gives a prize of cosmetic plastic surgery. The dictionary has a new word to describe those who take their references for a full and rich life from tabloid journalism: *wannabes*. Wannabes appear to ignore the negative longer term impact of pursuing their dreams in the public eye when life is not sunny all the time. They're victims of celebrity consumerism, which takes its toll on their natural energy.

He slept on the idea, then again, then again. After a week or so, he decided to invest the money in his company. Why? Ken decided that such an ostentatious show of new wealth wouldn't sit with his values, and that at a time when colleagues and customers may be feeling squeezed, it was important not to throw his success in their faces.

Changing and challenging

Before setting off in pursuit of a new dream or goal, ask yourself this question: When I achieve my dream, how will it impact my life? If the dream enhances your values, you find it easier to follow through into powerful action. If your goal causes you value conflicts, you're unlikely to be successful, so consider now why you want this result and decide whether the goal needs to be changed, postponed, or dropped.

Make yourself aware of the effect your success in any endeavour would have on you. The following framework is based on Neuro-linguistic Programming trainer Robert Dilts's model of the logical levels (see Chapter 7). Use the framework to check out your dream choices.

✔ **Environment:** How will achieving your dream impact on the place where you live or work and the people you hang out with? Will you be better off and able to afford a better car or bigger house? Will you be spending more time with your family or less? Will you have more, better, different work colleagues, friends, or neighbours?

✔ **Behaviour:** Maybe you want to acquire a new skill like ballroom dancing or a foreign language. How will this affect your behaviour? Will you be confident in approaching new dance partners or will you be better at conversing with foreigners or fellow students in your hometown?

✔ **Capability:** Will the confidence you develop on the dance floor or the language lab spill over into other areas of your life? Finding out about anything new or achieving any new result can expand your comfort zone (see Chapter 9). How can you use the skills you develop to meet your goal to affect other areas of your life?

✔ **Values and beliefs:** In Chapter 5, you can read how your core values are the states you want to enjoy, and your beliefs are your 'rules' about what things lead to. How will achieving your dream sit with your current values and beliefs? Will it stretch them (usually a good thing), conflict with them (always a bad thing), or honour them (guaranteed to make you feel good).

✔ **Identity:** Will achieving your dream reinforce or challenge your sense of who you are or your mission in life? Either is acceptable, but think about the dream's effect on identity so that you don't unwittingly sabotage your success to presevrve your identity status quo, and so that you're happy with the person you become in achieving your dream.

If you prepare in this way, you clear the ground for success and ensure that you're fully aligned with the new you, the one who's achieved the success you're aiming for, no matter how large or specific your objective.

Following the Six-Step Guaranteed Success Formula

In Chapter 3, we introduce the Guaranteed Success Formula. The following sections help you apply the formula to achieving your goal.

Step 1: Decide on your objective

Make your goal statement as simple and unambiguous as you can. What's the precise result you're after?

State your goal positively and in the present tense. For example, if you want to lose weight, state 'I weigh in at 140 pounds' rather than 'I want to lose 60 pounds'. Also decide what has to happen or be delivered for you to know that you've attained your goal; for example, 'I am wearing a new business suit with a 30-inch waist that fits neatly.'

Many goals have a built-in deadline (deliver the speech on such and such a date.) Decide immediately on a realistic yet challenging deadline for you to achieve your goal, and write that down.

You may see that you need to work through several stages. If so, set deadlines for them all. So, if you weigh 200 pounds today and your goal is to achieve an ideal weight of 140 pounds over a year, that would equate to a healthy loss of five pounds per month. You can set up monthly target weights to drop to 195 pounds for the first month, 190 pounds for the second, 185 pounds for the third and so on. If you plan to watch what you eat *and* increase your daily exercise, you can set intermediate goals for that too, steadily building up the distance you walk or jog over many weeks. This gives you a sense of perspective and keeps you on track from day one until you achieve your goal.

In goal setting, aim to keep as much control as possible over what needs to happen. If your objective depends on other people doing most of the work, you may quickly become frustrated and give up if they won't get on with it. This is an easy trap for managers or team players, so take care to set personal performance goals that *you* can achieve on your own, even when you're contributing to a bigger project.

Step 2: Create your plan

Decide what has to happen for you to attain your goal. Project planning is a well-developed business discipline, so whether the goal you're working on is simple or complex, you can strengthen your plan by following a few rules:

- ✔ **Establish your parameters.** You've already done this by writing down the specific objective and setting deadlines (see the previous section). If your aim is longer term, over several months or years, then set intermediate goals and deadlines.

- ✔ **Define your deliverables.** For some goals, you need many things to happen on the way to a final result. Distinguish between what absolutely must happen, or be delivered, and what would be a 'nice to have' that isn't essential. If your goal or dream is ambitious, then you probably do well to concentrate solely on the essentials because these essentials are going to take all your attention and effort.

    Also, you have to achieve some things before you can complete or begin other things, so you need to understand the best order of events. Give some thought to this and write everything down.

- ✔ **Set your milestones.** When you were a child, did you plague your parents on long car journeys by incessantly asking whether you were nearly at your destination? Children do this because they've no concept of milestones. To them, every journey involves an interminable period of waiting before finally the end shows up. Adults know that all journeys or tasks involve periods of time and effort that you can predict and manage.

    As you create your plan, think about the milestones or landmarks you can expect and that will confirm that things are working out according to plan. These markers give you feedback so that you know whether your plan is working or whether you need to think again and change things. For example, if you're learning to dance, a milestone would be to attend a dance and take to the floor for one or two key dances. The next milestone may be to add two more dances to your repertoire. A further milestone could be to have the confidence to ask someone who isn't your regular partner to dance with you at an event.

Write down your plan and share it with others. Writing down even a first draft forces you to get clear on the points in the previous bullets and exposes any conflicts or inconsistencies in your thinking, almost forcing you to resolve them. It creates something that you can share with others to get the benefit of their experience and advice, and it establishes a clear version of the future as you see it before you begin.

Our coaching clients develop and share their plans with us so that we can support them to make their plans happen. Sometimes, they ask us to hold them accountable for the commitments they made. At other times, simply telling another person what they plan to do is enough to build momentum.

Step 3: Put your plan into action

Time you spend planning is rarely wasted, even if the resulting plan changes several times over the course of reaching your goal. Any plan is better than no plan, and a well thought-through plan is better, but don't overdo the planning and fall into analysis paralysis. (Adopt the 80/20 principle; see Chapter 8.)

The action you take achieves your objectives, so following through with good implementation actions is the key to goal-achievement growth and success.

Whatever you've decided is your first step, take it immediately! If your first action is to tell someone about your new commitment, call the person up and tell her straight away. If you need to get weighed to establish your starting weight, jump on those scales now! Then take every subsequent action on time and in the way you visualised and planned it.

Step 4: Notice what happens as a result

You may like to throw yourself into new activities with heart and soul and not look up until the finish line is in sight. This works well with small or simple tasks but is a poor strategy for achieving anything that takes longer than a day or two. Decide up front how often to review your progress, and ensure that you take the time to do this properly.

Milestones (see Step 2) provide a natural place to take stock.
Don't just measure where you are or log when you achieve
the sub-objective. Reflect and review your experience, noting
what contributed to the peaks and troughs. Feed this information forward to reduce uncertainty in the rest of your plan.

You may see that you need to change some deadlines, break
some tasks down into smaller chunks and/or include new,
unplanned activities. You may even decide that your plan can
never achieve your objective and that you need to go back
to the drawing board to create a new plan in the light of your
experience.

Step 5: Change your approach

Whatever your experience tells you, adapt your approach as
necessary. This critical step renders failure obsolete. Even if
you have to go back to the start, use your recent experience
to create a far more robust strategy for achieving the objective. In most cases, though, starting over isn't necessary and
you can modify your approach while leaving most of the plan
and the milestones intact.

Step 6: Repeat the cycle until you achieve your result

Having changed your approach, renew your commitment and
get straight back into powerful, planned action. This is Step 3,
and you simply cycle through Steps 4 and 5 at every milestone
or review point until you achieve your goal.

The Guaranteed Success Formula ensures that you think
things through before you start and follow through to achieve
the result you want efficiently and easily. This works because
you already know how to achieve the result you seek; you just
need to act powerfully and confidently to bring it off.

No dream is too big for you with the Guaranteed Success
Formula. Notice how liberating it feels when you know that
you can't fail.

Part IV

Engaging Other People

The 5th Wave   By Rich Tennant

Now don't be nervous.
I heard this guy
has a huge ego,
but don't let
him intimidate
you.

In this part . . .

Y ou look at how to flex your increased personal power at work and in your private life so you stand tall and strong. Specifically, you look at what you can do at work and take on a new approach to romance, even getting the impossible date of your dreams. You also see how to take the plunge into social media.

Chapter 13

Demonstrating Confidence in the Workplace

*T*he most confident version of you will be immediately recognisable in the workplace. You'll be at ease with yourself and other people, straightforward and generous in your dealings with your fellow workers, cooperative and pleasant to work with, ready to laugh at the odd joke, and *very* effective in getting your job done.

So, now is the time to consider how you are in your place of work, and to apply your confidence in your job. This chapter helps you explore your relation to your work and the impact this relationship has on your confidence. You find many ways to increase your confidence and be able to use this confidence to your advantage both in your work and in other parts of your life.

Developing Confidence in Your Professional Life

When you're introduced to someone new, and they ask you the age-old question, 'And what do you do?' how do you answer? So much of your sense of who you are is bound up in your work that the description you offer is a powerful indicator of the meaning that work has in your life and the degree of success you can expect.

Your workplace gives you a constant bombardment of influences, both positive and negative, from the physical environment, the people in it, the tempo and nature of the work, and how closely you identify with what is getting done.

Keep in mind that maintaining an attitude that helps you to get everything you need from your work is your responsibility: including a confident sense of pride and wellbeing from doing your job well.

Realising that your job isn't you

Although you may protest that your job doesn't bear any direct relation to who you really are, what is important to you, or what you want to achieve in your life, it nonetheless exerts a powerful influence on your sense of identity. Holding down a job that seems at odds with your true sense of self in the world is possible, but unusual, and takes a lot of confidence and self-belief.

Hating your job, or your employer, can become a drag on your deeper beliefs about yourself and your value in the world. Taking action with confidence from this position is particularly difficult because you've so little affinity with who you're being when you're working and where this is leading you.

But your *work* isn't the same thing as your *job*. Your work can be a much fuller expression of your values and beliefs about yourself than any single job can be, even a good job that suits you. Your work in the world can be something close to your spirit, something almost sacred. But to find your true work, you have to be prepared to think beyond the job you're doing.

A work-based sense of self

Some people hold onto a role-based sense of self in the face of an enormous weight of contrary evidence. Nicky, for example, is an actress who has spent only two or three years out of the last 10 working in this role. In between times, she's spent many years doing temporary office jobs, waiting on tables in restaurants, or having no job and no income at all. And yet she feels and acts the part of 'actress', albeit one who is temporarily doing something else. The 'actress' part of her self-image is her role identity; the temporary work is what she has to do to pay her bills.

When she goes to parties, as she does often, how do you think she answers the question 'what do you do? 'Does she tell people that she does 'pretty much anything to make ends meet'? Of course not: she tells people she is an actress, and if we haven't seen her recently on television, we know that this career choice includes periods of enforced idleness and probably temporary jobs. Neither she nor we are particularly concerned about her other jobs (even though she spends 75 per cent of her time doing them) because they express little or nothing about who she is as a person and what her life is about.

The place to start is with you. This book can help you to think out your true sense of who you are, perhaps at a deeper level than you've ever thought about it before. As you increase your self-knowledge, you're in a far better position to decide upon the work you want to do in the world. Then, as you make the changes you find necessary, you become far more confident and better able to live powerfully a life that is balanced and fulfilling.

Defining your professional identity

If you're a lawyer, or a medical doctor, then in the absence of any other information about you, people can reasonably accurately assume a whole lot of things about your ethics, values, social standing, and so on. They can make these assumptions because your identity in society is defined by the work you do. For members of the professions, the magic is in the job title; it defines them to themselves and to others.

If you're not a member of a recognised profession, you don't have all the accoutrements of a professional identity. But it's recognising that you do a professional job that people need and value is still essential. In order to feel and act with total confidence, you must get clear about the contribution of the work you do and how it fits into the wider value chain in your organisation and beyond into society.

Try drawing a diagram of your job in its broadest context; like Figure 13-1, filling in the details. No job operates independently of everything else, so think about how your role at work fits into the greater scheme of things in your business. Does your company make something, or provide a service that enables other people to do their work? Perhaps you help to maintain the home or work environment that enables other people to do their work. All these things are essential for the economy to be successful.

Include and think about everything you can take pride in around your work. Do you work alone or in a team? (Both need special qualities.) Do you supervise other people, do you work remotely from the main office, do you work in the home providing care for your family to allow them to engage fully in the world? All these roles are essential for a healthy society.

Uncovering what you want to do

Of course, that you can step straight into the work of your dreams is unlikely. You need to build up your skills and experience, make the contacts, gain the profile, and earn the opportunity to make the break. This process is quite normal; but if you've no sense of these things, if you cannot see your way ever to getting the work you want, then you've a problem that you need to deal with.

At its highest, your *work* in the world is an expression of your being; something powerful and close to your core. But your job doesn't automatically give you the opportunity to do your chosen work. You need to manage this situation: take steps to acquire the skills you need and balance your life with voluntary work closer to your ideal as you take the time to develop your career.

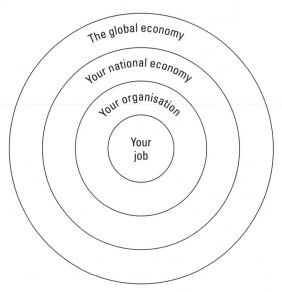

The global economy

Your national economy

Your organisation

Your job

Figure 13-1: The broader context of your work.

Answer the following questions to get a clearer vision of your ideal work:

✔ **What do you absolutely love about working?** This question is an unusual one, and you may, like many people when asked it, find it easier to come up with an immediate list of what you don't like about working. Persevere; you'll find that you love many things about working, from a reason to go to town, to the great friends you work with, from the interesting people you meet, to the problems you get to solve, and so on.

Don't stop thinking until you've written down four or five things, even if they're not available in your current job role.

✔ **What aspects of your work are you really good at, or have other people told you that you're really good at?** Wow! Include all the things that you know you're good at, even if nobody else does. Perhaps you're a good timekeeper, or maybe you're sensitive and caring when your co-workers are feeling down. Perhaps you're good at dealing with the boss, or the customers, or maybe you're excellent at getting on with the job without being distracted. Stretch your thinking and go for four or five things.

✔ **What is absolutely essential for you to have available in your work?** This question is a great one to ask yourself, whether or not you believe your current role gives you what you need. You may include things like meeting people, good money, being part of a team, or the opportunity to find out new things, or the chance to make a real difference.

Think about what *you* need. How much of it would be available in your current role if you came at it a little differently?

✔ **What do you feel you really ought or would like to be doing?** Many people who want to change jobs lack clarity in their ideas about the work they wish they were doing. So, what is it for you? How much more of the things you really need would be available in the job you would prefer to be doing?

✔ **Finally, what is the truth that your answers whisper to you?** Bring all your other answers to mind. Should you be doing something else? Would it make any difference? Other than giving you more money, do you have clear insight into how you can ensure that your next role supports you better?

After answering all these questions, you have a clearer idea than ever before of how you see your work in the world and what about it is most important to you. Now you need to look at the kind of jobs you've been doing. Have they given you what you need? Will they ever? When your work aligns with your values, you can be fully confident and fully empowered in your job. What do you need to change to make it so?

This powerful exercise can help you get in touch with your deeper need for work. You're most powerful and confident in your work when you're able to find jobs and roles that match your developing sense of vocation and purpose.

Finding value in what you do

Uncovering the hidden value in your work is important for your self-respect and contributes to your confidence.

Whether what you do is something you simply fell into, or whether it was a planned and conscious choice, your job defines you in the world more than almost anything else. You should always ask yourself what is valuable about the work you do in the larger scheme of things, and be sure that you bring to mind all the hidden value.

If you work for a large company or a well-known branded business, you can take pride in that. Maybe you work for the government, or the local authority. Take a pride in that. If you work with children, or with sick people, or people with special needs, you may also have some sense of vocation and you can take pride in that.

Whatever you do, take pride in your professionalism. *Professionalism* is about knowing what needs to be done and going about it competently. When you adopt a professional approach to your work, you demonstrate your confidence to other people that you know what you're doing, which in turn inspires them to be confident in you.

Eleanor Roosevelt said that the future belongs to those who believe in the beauty of their dreams. A key to confidence is having dreams. Connecting your work with your growing sense of your life's purpose and your dreams is a powerful means to having that work sing to your soul.

Becoming Assertive

The key to effective communication and relationships with most colleagues in your organisation (including your boss) is a set of personal skills that are usually lumped together and called assertiveness. Assertiveness is one of those acquired skills you need training and practice to acquire.

Assertiveness specialist coaches claim that this skills set is more powerful than any other in business. It can protect and boost your self-esteem, build your confidence, and reduce your stress levels.

Assertive people are generally liked and respected, they respond well in tight spots, and they aren't afraid to say 'no'. You know where you are with an assertive person; they don't get put upon.

So what is this miracle skills set called assertiveness? At its core, *assertiveness* is the conviction that every person is equal to every other and that each person has the responsibility to take care of his or her personal needs and rights. This statement includes an implicit acceptance that this applies to all of us, so in claiming it for yourself you also claim it on behalf of all your colleagues.

The fundamentals of assertiveness are:

- ✔ You value yourself and others as equals.

- ✔ You have the ability to say 'yes' or 'no' to anyone when you choose, and you do not always choose to offer a reason for it.

- ✔ You embrace and protect your human rights. You stand up for yourself and you're unafraid to be known for doing so.

- ✔ You take responsibility for your own needs and ensure that you have them met.

- ✔ You take responsibility for your own contribution and the value you create. You aren't afraid to admit to mistakes nor to ask for help when you need it.

- ✔ You express your thoughts and feelings honestly, whether positive or negative, and with due respect for others.

- ✔ You're able to handle conflict when it arises. You're prepared to confront difficult people when necessary or appropriate.

- ✔ You give and receive feedback honestly and in a straightforward manner. You take the trouble to do so effectively and completely.

- ✔ You respect these rights in others and understand that they've the same rights as you.

Don't worry if you don't feel that you match up to all these points yet. First, knowing what they are is important. As you grow in confidence from working with this book, you'll naturally become more assertive and powerful.

Showing Confidence in Specific Work Situations

Several common work situations may test your confidence. This section offers advice on how to manage your confidence in meetings and during presentations.

You can develop new skills, or *competencies* as they're often called in business, through training and practice. Nothing in business is impossible to master (certainly nothing is as difficult as finding out how to walk and talk, and most of us manage that).

If your employer is asking you to do something for which you don't yet have the requisite skill, you should insist on the training. And if you find yourself struggling with any task at work, your first question should always be: How can I acquire the skill to do this task better or faster? This approach takes you forward into growth and confidence, rather than shrinking backward into fear and avoidance.

Demonstrating power and presence in meetings

Have you ever sat in a meeting just bursting to make a telling point only to find that the discussion has moved on before you're able to get it in? Or have you come up with a brilliant idea after the meeting is over and felt if only you could go back in time and make the point everyone would acknowledge you for solving the problem or pointing up the unnoticed flaw in the argument? If you have, then congratulations, you're a fully functioning, normal human being. We've all done it.

The main cause of such missed opportunities is the lack of balance between the *two* conversations that are going on in the meeting: the one in the room and the one in your head. When you're fully *present and engaged* in the meeting conversation, the conversation in your head fades into the background where it belongs most of the time. When you're feeling nervous or self-conscious, however, the dialogue in your head becomes predominant and prevents you from being fully engaged in the meeting.

 You may feel self-conscious just because you're in unfamiliar territory. Take a few deep breaths (from your abdomen, as we explain in Chapter 11) to ease the tension, focus on who is in the room and the details of what they're wearing, just to bring yourself fully into the present.

Understand that this situation is normal, and ease up on yourself. Accept that the more natural you can be in the meeting situation, the more balance you achieve between your inner and outer dialogues.

If you can become curious about how the external conversation is developing and how the meeting will turn out, you'll find yourself naturally focused on the outer discussion. From this position, your own ideas and comments come up more naturally and more appropriately, making your points is easier and you grow in confidence.

Above all, relax. Whether the meeting is highly formal and large, or small and routine, the more engaged you become in the business of the meeting, the more effective your contribution becomes.

Shining during presentations

A whole chapter of this book, Chapter 11, is dedicated to helping you find your voice in the world and expressing yourself in the most powerful ways possible. Here, you can look at some of the skills you need to make powerful work presentations.

Making effective presentations, like most other things in your professional life, is an acquired skill. Nobody is a born orator, just as no one grows up being able to read a balance sheet or create a budget. In order to give effective presentations, you need to get proper instruction from a training course, books, or tapes. A wealth of material is available to help you. And while the subject is too big to go into much detail here, we offer a few of the key things that you need to bear in mind.

✔ Basic as it sounds, the first thing to ask yourself is 'what is my point?' Many beginners and even many experienced speakers forget that without a point their talk is quite literally pointless. People find it difficult to give a pointless talk with confidence and conviction. So determine your point of view and what you want your audience to do as a result of hearing what you have to say.

✔ Next, ask who you're talking to. You need to know the composition of your audience before you can start to think about how to pitch your talk. Are they knowledgeable or novices in your subject? Do you have to spell things out for them or can you assume that they know what you're talking about, jargon included?

After you consider the basics, turn yourself to the vexed question of whether you need slides. Just because a projector is available, or even habitual, consider whether slides would really add anything to your message (getting the audience's attention off you and giving yourself a crib-sheet to read off are not good enough reasons). If you decide to use a projector, follow these top guidelines:

✔ Your slides are there for your audience. Make sure that they're legible from the back of the room and that the information on them is crisp and to the point.

✔ Assume that your audience can read and don't treat your slides as cue cards. If you want your audience to take in what is written on the slide, shut up and let them read it.

✔ Unless you're a graphic artist, don't be tempted by fancy fonts or colour schemes, any kind of animation, or even clip art. And use slide-builds sparingly. What looks great on your laptop when you're preparing, all too often looks awful when projected onto a big screen.

✔ Always test your presentation on the actual equipment you'll be using. Never, ever attempt to use external links to the Internet or to some kind of live demonstration unless you're a specialist, and even then only with caution.

✔ Have a contingency plan in case your equipment fails or won't behave itself. Have copies of the slides to hand out, but don't hand them out before you speak unless you don't mind people flicking through the pack while you're talking.

✔ Rehearse, rehearse, and rehearse. Time yourself and get your script down onto a few cue cards. This activity ensures that you're confident in what you're going to say, and in your timings.

Always bear in mind the golden rules of technology when making any kind of presentation involving projection or sound equipment: *what can go wrong will go wrong* sooner or later, and *less is more* in the balance of complexity versus clarity. Keep things simple and allow yourself the chance to connect with your audience.

You improve your skills most effectively through practice and feedback. So seek out opportunities in non-work situations to hone your developing skills. Adult education classes in local colleges, women's groups, and your local church are always on the lookout for speakers. Offer yourself up for the experience and do your developing where you won't have to live with the consequences.

Rejecting manipulation and bullying

Bullying is all too common in the workplace. Surveys show that millions of people feel bullied every day at work, which takes a heavy toll on confidence. If you feel you're a victim of serious bullying at work, seek professional help from your HR or union representative, or perhaps your functional director. Bullying is never acceptable, by anyone, in any circumstances.

While the unacceptability of bullying is perfectly clear in cases of physical intimidation or sexual and racial harassment, the less dramatic, lower-intensity form of bullying by shouting, verbal abuse, and manipulation can sap your self-esteem just as surely as a flagrant assault.

The manipulative bully's techniques include sarcasm, unjustified criticism, trivial faultfinding and humiliation, especially in front of others. It can also include your being overruled, isolated, and otherwise excluded from team activities. All these things are calculated to sap your self-confidence to make you more of a target.

You protect yourself best by refusing to play the victim. Recognise that the bully is the one who is inadequate and needs fixing, not you. Don't be taken in by criticism, even though it may have a grain of truth in it. No amount of improvement in your performance will satisfy your bully; a bully isn't interested in improving you, only in having control over you.

If you seem to attract such people either into your professional or your private life, it may be because you exhibit certain personality traits that mark you as a target for someone with a bullying personality. *This is not your fault.* Table 13-1 contains practical tips on how to offset tendencies that make you easy prey for bully boys (and girls).

Table 13-1   Personality Traits and Being Bullied

Tendency	*Counter Behaviours*
You want to please.	Accept that you will never be able to please everyone, especially a bully.
You take on more and more to gain approval.	Set yourself sensible limits.
You find it hard to say 'no'.	Find out how to be more assertive.
You've a strong desire to think well of others.	Be more objective; ask others' opinions.
You want things to be perfect.	Realise that perfection isn't possible and turn to Chapter 8.
You've a strong need to feel valued.	Discover how to value yourself (see Chapter 5).
You tend to discount your own contributions.	Ask yourself whether what you're expected to do is fair and reasonable.

Your first step in dealing successfully with a bully is to take control. Acknowledge your need to be more assertive, and look at that section in this chapter. You can almost certainly do something to stop yourself being victimised. Consider the following actions. Don't think for too long though – you need to take decisive action quickly:

✔ Let your union or staff representative know about the problem. Take any advice they offer you, and if this advice is inadequate check out any helplines or consult your local Citizen's Advice Bureau.

✔ Talk about the situation to your colleagues (if they will discuss it). Find out whether anyone else is suffering and whether other people are aware of what is happening to you. Others may be suffering in silence.

✔ Start a diary and keep a written record of all incidents. You may need this detailed evidence later if things come to a head but more likely it acts as a strong disincentive on your bully.

✔ Confront your bully in person if you feel you can, otherwise do it by email or memo. In firm but non-aggressive language, make it clear what you're objecting to in their behaviour. Keep a copy and any reply. This action may end their bullying.

✔ If you decide to make a formal complaint, take advice first from HR or your union and follow your company's procedures. Ask your representatives to help you; this support will cut down greatly on the stress on you.

If you've made a formal complaint, be aware that your bully's job may now be in jeopardy. You need to be able to substantiate your allegations through witnesses or written records, and you may have to confront your bully in an investigation.

If you're not satisfied by the outcome of the internal investigation, take advice on your legal rights. If you leave your job and subsequently make a claim to an employment tribunal, they will expect you to have first tried to resolve the situation using the internal procedures. Any records you have will be heard when the tribunal hears your claim.

Managing Your Boss

Complaints about the boss are commonplace in work life and pretty much inevitable. Remembering that however big and scary your boss may appear to you now, he got that way by having to cope with difficult situations on his own and that underneath he is as vulnerable as you are, can help your confidence.

The bottom line with bosses is that they need to get the job done and meet their performance targets. They need their team members to perform effectively and they've strategies for getting the required performance out of their subordinates.

When the pressure is on, bosses become anxious and scared just like anyone else, and those occasions are when problems often show up.

Anyone who is persistently out of sorts or bad tempered is almost certainly stressed and needs help whether they know it or not. You may feel that you can do nothing to help your boss with his issues, but you can certainly manage your own.

Dealing with feedback

Finding out how to manage feedback is important for your self-confidence. If you can receive and give feedback effectively, and especially turn even poorly delivered feedback to your advantage, you can grow massively in confidence and effectiveness at work.

Figure 13-2 shows an example of ineffective feedback to a secretary who fails to use the spell checker in her word processor.

Figure 13-3 offers a more professional and effective way of giving feedback that may actually result in a change for the better.

The next sections offer tips for giving and getting feedback.

Giving effective feedback

When giving feedback, whether positive or negative, things generally go most smoothly if you follow a few simple rules:

- ✔ **Be clear about the information you're imparting and own the responsibility of making the point.** You don't want any grey areas at the end, and you want to make sure that your receiver knows that this clear information is coming from you.

- ✔ **Focus on the action you want to take place.** Describe the facts of the situation and how you want the other person to change. Don't judge or offer opinions about why the problem is arising – you may get it wrong.

✔ **Be as specific as possible.** Take a keyhole or laser surgery approach to your intervention. Deal as precisely as possible with the situation and avoid generalisations like *always* and *never*. If your feedback deals with some aspect of behaviour, ensure that you address the behaviour and not the character of the person.

✔ **Emphasise the positive aspects of the situation.** This emphasis helps the person receiving your input to keep his receiving channels open. If you're correcting an error or making another point that he may receive as criticism, it can be helpful to the receiver if you sandwich the negative point between something positive, both before and after. This approach is not manipulative if you do it honestly, and is helpful to the person who has to take your point on board.

Joan, you've left typos in the weekly review again.

Sorry Mrs Farrell.

Why do you think you have a spell checker? All you have to do is use it and it will find most of them for you?

Sorry Mrs Farrell.

The problem is it makes us all look slip-shod. The work you put out damages the image of the whole department; it reflects badly on me.

Sorry Mrs Farrell.

Yes, well you say you're sorry every time we have this conversation and nothing ever changes. It simply isn't good enough and you are going to have to change. If you don't mend your ways my girl this is going to end in tears, yours. Is that clear?

Yes Mrs Farrell.

Well let this be the last time, or else. I mean it.

Sorry Mrs Farrell.

Figure 13-2: How *not* to give feedback.

Joan, thank you very much for the weekly review. Once again you have turned it around very quickly and efficiently.

Thank you Mrs Farrell.

I know we have talked about this before but there are still some typos. Are you having problems using the spell-checker?

Err, yes, I keep forgetting.

Why don't you put a sticky label on the side of the computer to remind you about spell-checking your work and then it will stop happening. It is so easy to use.

Okay Mrs Farrell, I'll definitely do that.

Good Joan; if you need any further training on the system, let me know and I can organise it.

Thank you, I will do.

Once again Joan, thank you for this.

Figure 13-3: Giving effective feedback.

Turning negative feedback around

Input from your boss that you receive as criticism, nit-picking, or nagging is just an inadequate form of feedback. The information it contains may be valuable to you though, and important to your organisation, so understanding what your boss is trying to communicate is worthwhile.

If you can see that your boss's criticism of you is just his inadequate way of giving you information, you retain more power in the relationship. You can do two things that may surprise him and turn things around:

✓ Take on board any feedback that may be useful to you in improving your performance and let your boss know what this feedback is.

✓ Ask permission to give your boss feedback on how he can communicate with *you* more effectively. If you do this, follow all the rules on being specific, focusing on the action, and so on from the preceding 'Giving effective feedback' section. Remember, you both share the goal of improving performance.

Getting your boss to keep his promises

The frustration of being offered some benefit or reward but not receiving it can corrupt your relationship with your employer and erode your confidence.

Unfulfilled promises generally fall into one of two cases:

- ✔ **Case 1:** You believe that your boss has promised you something that he didn't. He may be surprised that you feel a promise has been made.

- ✔ **Case 2:** You both know full well that the promise has been made and yet action is being delayed for reasons that have not been made clear to you.

In both cases, you feel maligned or abused and your self-esteem and self-confidence is going to suffer unless you do something about it.

At the root of both cases is a problem with communication. In Case 1, you may have unintentionally translated a good intention by your boss into a promise. In Case 2, the ambiguity may be deliberate. Your boss may simply have made the promise to keep you quiet without intending to fulfil it any time soon. Fortunately, the remedy for both is simple and is the same action.

What you do, as a professional person of integrity, is put down in writing in the form of an email or memo any important exchanges. In clear and straightforward language, write down what you believe has been agreed. Figure 13-4 gives an example.

Dear Boss

Thanks for seeing me yesterday to discuss my pay rise. I'm obviously delighted that you have agreed to my request and I'm looking forward to receiving it. When will this be by the way? (This is the first question my wife will ask me). Do please confirm a date and let me know if there is going to be any delay.

Thanks and regards

Figure 13-4: Putting an understanding in writing.

Of course, if you've the presence of mind in the discussion to ask when the reward is to take effect, you already know the promised date and you can include it in your note.

How will your boss react to this written input? In the majority of cases, your note simply confirms what your boss agreed to do, and your confirmation acts as a reminder. If you send it as an email, your boss can forward it to his PA, HR, or payroll with a confirmation that he has agreed to your note and a request for action. Then it will be done – easy for everyone.

But what happens when your boss doesn't agree or doesn't take action? In the case of a misunderstanding, your note is likely to evoke an immediate response from your boss pointing up the mismatch. Will he be annoyed? Maybe, a little bit, as the issue has returned so quickly, but you're far better to identify his mistake in communication immediately and give him the chance to rectify it. You can apologise if necessary to maintain rapport, and immediately ask when you can expect the reward. If he can't give you any indication, then he is probably fobbing you off, which is Case 2.

So what will be your boss's reaction to your note if he is using delaying tactics? You catch him out and force his hand. If he continues to be evasive, then you know that he is simply stringing you along. You don't have your reward, but you do have your integrity restored. You may be annoyed, but it won't be directed at yourself. You may use your annoyance to give you the motivation to do something about changing your dishonest boss by changing your job.

Telling your boss he's wrong

At the heart of confidence is trust: trust in yourself, trust in other people, and trust that things will turn out okay. Telling your boss that he's wrong requires that you feel all three, so you need to take a look at the structure and dynamics of the situation.

First, bear in mind that neither you nor your boss is infallible. Everyone makes mistakes from time to time; everyone makes errors of fact and judgement. Making mistakes is perfectly human. What matters most in business is what you do to remedy the immediate problem and what you can then do to stop the situation occurring again.

If you're sure that you're correct about your boss's error or misjudgement, then you owe it to him to point it out before the damage gets worse. You need trust in yourself here. No matter what gap there may be in age, prestige, salary, experience, or levels in the hierarchy, you're just as valuable a human being as your boss and you owe it to him, person to person, to point out the error. If you do so with respect and a little care (for example, not in front of your colleagues or in the middle of a meeting), your boss will remember and respect you for your honesty and tact.

If you've some evidence ready to support your judgement that he has made an error, use it discreetly. It can help your boss to come to terms with his error more quickly but spare his blushes with other people. If you point out your boss's errors in public, he won't thank you for it.

If you've an honest and straightforward remedy, offer it to help fix his mistake quickly. Don't become wedded to your solution, though, as he may choose another.

Fundamentally, being assertive and acting to inform your boss of the error is what counts. You can grow in confidence from your taking the action and so, if he is any good as a leader at all, can your boss.

Casting Off Your Cloak of Invisibility

More often than not, the reason nobody is acknowledging the great job you're doing is because your superiors and colleagues are too busy worrying about their own performances. Don't be afraid to seize the opportunity to take powerful action to bring your excellent work to the attention of your boss and colleagues.

The following formula creates a winning situation for everyone. If you use it, you set yourself apart as the one in a thousand employees who cares enough about performance to take it on.

Follow these steps:

1. **Ask your boss to define exactly what he wants from you in order for you to get a five-star annual appraisal.**

   The more detailed this definition is, the better. Get him to spell out, from his point of view, what *good* looks like, then play it back: 'So if I do this, this, and this, and avoid that and that, you will think I'm doing an excellent job, right?' When you have agreement, write it down (but don't send it anywhere just yet).

2. **Ask the same question of other people who depend on you or are affected by your performance.**

   These people may be customers or a group of colleagues who use your output in some significant way. Find out, from their perspective, what *good* looks like, play it back, get their agreement, and write it down for your own use later.

3. **Pull it all together into job objectives that you can realistically achieve.**

   You've a lot of detailed input on how other people depend on you and what they need you to do well in order to be happy with your performance.

4. **Spell out what you feel you can reliably deliver to your boss, colleagues, and customers.**

   Present them with a document that outlines the objectives you're committed to achieving (perhaps with training or some other assistance) and get their agreement to it (you may need to negotiate and compromise).

Doing the work to put together an action plan helps you achieve a number of really important objectives:

- ✔ Composing a job specification that is relevant, detailed, achievable, and creates value.

- ✔ Letting your boss and colleagues know what to expect from you and that they can rely on you to deliver.

- ✔ Laying a solid basis for renegotiating expectations and outcomes should anything change.

You've a perfect right, a duty even, to check in with your colleagues periodically to ensure that they're happy with your performance. And each time you do so it reminds them of what a good and dependable job you do.

Dealing Confidently with Corporate Change

As change managers know, change tends to trigger a cycle of reactions and feelings. These reactions and feelings fall into a sequence of predictable stages, irrespective of whether the change is planned or unplanned. Figure 13-5 shows a simple change curve.

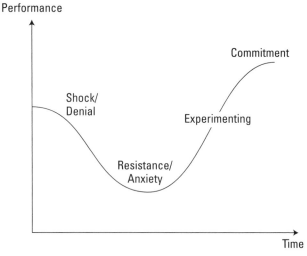

Figure 13-5: Changing with the change curve.

The time you spend at each stage and the intensity of your reaction depends on your personality and the nature of the change. To make a successful transition, however, you have to work through all the stages. The stages are:

1. **Shock or Denial:** At this initial response, your natural response may be to minimise the impact of the change by trivialising it or denying that it exists.

2. **Resistance and Anxiety:** This stage is characterised by your strong emotions and also feelings of flatness, accompanied often by a loss of confidence. You may have difficulties in coping with the new circumstances, which makes it hard to accept the changes.

3. **Experimenting:** Activity now increases as you test new ways and approaches towards the change. You may have firm ideas of how things should be in relation to the new situation and feel frustration as the inevitable mistakes are made.

4. **Commitment:** By this stage, you have adopted new behaviour and accepted the change. You're working well and confidently with the new situation. You may reflect on how and why things are different, and attempt to understand all the emotion and activity of the previous stages.

Getting through rejection

One of the messages coaches give out loud and clear is that a normal part of growth is *not* to be chosen for every role or assignment. If you set out your stall to be successful, then you need to be prepared to grow from the experience of being rejected from time to time. Often, a valid reason exists and you can benefit from the disappointment.

One of the most valuable approaches to rejection is to embrace change and disappointments from the mind-set that they simply represent feedback rather than failure. For every company that wins a piece of work, several others lose the work. For every successful candidate at an interview, a number get a rejection call.

The rejection is not about you as a person, but about your skills and style not being appropriate at this time for this company or customer.

Winners stay professional and persist for the long term. Confident people welcome feedback and continue to grow.

Taking on tips for job interviews

In any situation in life, you can be more confident if you know what to expect and you feel well prepared.

A job interview isn't something you experience all that often, so take advantage of the many books and any training you're offered to help you interview well.

Even the most mundane of jobs often attract many more applications than the employer can easily handle. In the initial sifting phase, almost any excuse is used to disqualify a CV or résumé from the pile of applications, so if you're called for interview, congratulate yourself for being one of the few to get through this sift.

The interview itself is structured in simple stages:

1. The first few minutes are all about establishing the channel of communication, or *rapport*.

2. You need to listen actively as the interviewer outlines key information about the organisation and the job.

3. The attention turns to you next as you and the interviewer investigate how your particular mix of capability, experience, and aspiration can generate value in the job.

4. A short closing-down phase enables you to ask any remaining questions.

This process is the ideal with a trained HR professional. The interviewer's task is to eliminate candidates who won't help to create the value the company is looking to generate.

Above all, make sure that you're *never* guilty of these top confidence-related reasons for rejection at interview stage:

✔ **Lack of planning:** Being unable to express clear purpose and goals.

✔ **Passive and indifferent behaviour:** Failing to express interest and enthusiasm; lack of vitality; poor eye contact.

✔ **Poor confidence and poise:** Appearing ill at ease and unduly nervous.

You've one further task as an interviewed candidate to set you apart from the pack. Within 24 hours, drop your interviewers a personal note thanking them for their time, and for being so helpful and informative. Confirm whether or not you remain interested in the post and, if you are, tell them you're looking forward to the next stage in the process. Don't revisit any of your answers or ask a further question at this stage. Your note is by way of a simple thank-you and confirmation to your interviewer, and doesn't require a reply. Not one in a hundred candidates shows this simple courtesy.

Taming the threat of redundancy

As it is jobs or roles that get made redundant, and not people, you can only be made redundant if you see yourself as your job. You may find yourself out of work for a while, and it certainly won't be of your choosing, but you avoid the quite ridiculous and yet soul-destroying label of being redundant yourself.

Fully embrace the notion of work being something you choose to do for yourself and sometimes – often – you pursue this work through a job role. Now you've a clear distinction between the work you've taken on in the world and the medium through which you're currently engaged in your work. This relationship is far healthier to your job and is one that enables you to have much more personal power.

The way forward is to hold on to who you are and your true purpose and find the work or lifestyle that fits for you right now. Hold on to the idea that this stage is merely a transition in your life. Confidence is about accepting and embracing the energy of the change and finding the positive lesson for you. Ask someone who has been made redundant six months after the event, and many will tell you that it was the best thing that happened to them – it gave them freedom to move on and was a catalyst for change.

The following is a good example: When the British heavy industries of coal mining and shipbuilding were closed down over a 20-year period, hundreds of thousands of workers lost their jobs. Many of these workers had been miners or shipbuilders all their lives, and their fathers before them. Their identity was bound up in being a miner, and because the government had no more use for miners it had no further use for them. Many saw themselves as literally without use and useless; they were finished. Many of them reached retirement age without ever working again.

In stark contrast, thousands of other workers took their redundancy pay and used it to build new lives, either starting their own businesses or moving away to parts of the country where there were more and different jobs.

The people who moved on saw the problem for what it was: their heavy-industry jobs were gone forever and they needed to find different kinds of jobs. The rest embraced prolonged unemployment with their proud industrial identities intact, but never worked again.

Chapter 14

Approaching Romantic Relationships with Confidence

A leading brand of chocolate confectionery used a single storyline in its TV advertising for over 25 years. Usually at night, a romantic action man, rugged and fashionable in black, is dropped from a helicopter into a raging torrent where he has to navigate the rapids before climbing 500 feet up a sheer cliff face, before climbing in through the window of a magnificent chateau and into the bedroom of a beautiful woman. He deposits a box of chocolates and a mystery visiting card by her bedside and immediately departs. He is doing it for no other reason than the lady loves the chocolates!

For your average man this standard is a high one to meet, and affairs of the heart test even the bravest. Romance seems to contain every ingredient of a fiendish confidence test: strong desire, fear of failure and humiliation and the despair of never succeeding. But on the other hand, when things just seem to 'click', romance seems the most natural thing in the world, an effortless joyride into lifelong relationship.

Doesn't it strike you as odd that nature takes such a chance with something so important as survival of the species? The truth is that these rituals of romantic relationship are not natural at all; society invented them, and you feel much more confident about negotiating them when you know how they work, and how they work on you.

Relating with Romance

So what does romance mean to you? Originally *a romance* was a mediaeval tale, in song or verse, told about some chivalrous hero (like knights rescuing damsels about to be consumed by fire-breathing dragons). Key characteristics of such tales were that they were fantastic, removed from everyday life and yet moving. Whether they were really true wasn't the point. What was important was that they transported their listeners to a better, higher realm of human nature and put them in touch with the heroic in their own lives.

Several hundred years later, you seek exactly the same thing when you go to the cinema or watch something romantic on TV. Human nature doesn't seem to have changed much in that time: What has changed is the medium through which you satisfy your innate need for romance.

Checking in on cultural notions of romance

The influences and trends in society that shape beliefs and expectations are popularly known as *culture*. A good working definition of culture is 'the way we do things around here'. Or rather, the way we are *supposed* to do things, because the conventions and fashions embedded within culture may not be consistently observed.

While you're free to accept or reject the conventions your culture offers up to you, they remain influential in shaping how you think about things. Living comfortably outside cultural norms requires above-average energy, power and confidence.

You don't have to settle for less than you want in matters of romance, provided what you want is achievable and supports you in building the life you want. Your starting point is an examination of your current, perhaps unconscious views of what romance means to you.

As a five-minute test, go through the scenarios in the following list and ask yourself which of them you feel are romantic:

- ✔ Coming from rival dynasties, the couple is star-crossed from the start. They rail against their families, their friends, and society to be together. Reality catches up with them when they both die in a tragic accident while being pursued by their families.

- ✔ She is assigned as a live-in nanny to work with the widower's difficult children. She becomes their loving confidante, and despite the most difficult of circumstances and the widower's class consciousness, their shared love of the children eventually brings them together.

- ✔ She is beautiful and destined for an arranged marriage to an eligible socialite when she meets the man who introduces her to raw, real life for the first time. Desperately in love, he dies tragically, giving up his own life so that she may live on.

- ✔ A couple overcomes radically different religious and family backgrounds to forge a passionate and loving relationship based upon who they are as individuals. Eventually, though, their cultural differences prove overwhelming and they're forced apart.

- ✔ A couple become best friends over many years, helping each other through difficult times with other partners before they realise that they truly love each other and were meant to be together all along.

How many of these scenarios strike chords in you? The result doesn't matter so much as your awareness of some of the stereotypes that constantly shape our expectations. If you didn't already spot them, you may enjoy revisiting them looking for the lovers from *Romeo and Juliet, The Sound of Music, Titanic, The Way We Were,* and *When Harry Met Sally.*

Popular culture's representation of romantic love dictates that it be hard won, occur only after trials or near-fatal mistakes, and eventually flower against all the odds. It either ends happily or, just as frequently, gets snuffed out tragically and prematurely.

Would any sane person choose this way to conduct their most important personal relationship? And yet this raw material is fed to you to shape your concept of romantic relationships.

You can easily create your own list of favourite films, plays, and novels. Doing so is worthwhile as it tells you a lot about how culture has shaped your personal notions of romance. When you're done, ask yourself honestly, how does this compare with your real life?

Choosing your own view of romance

Despite being removed from real life, these fantastic, romantic stories exert a powerful influence on you through the media of film, TV, and novels. So, unless misery and pain are in your values hierarchy, you're going to benefit from taking control of what romance means to you from now on. This section helps you to do that and renders you better able to take those scary first steps.

Take a few minutes right now to identify the things you most want in a romantic, loving relationship, and make yourself a list of the top half-dozen.

It doesn't matter whether you were together for one evening or have been married for 20 years. Think about your romantic relationships right now and summarise one or two, in one paragraph, in totally dispassionate language, as in the following examples:

- ✔ When we got together, our respective friends were amazed. We were so different from each other and so different from our partners in previous relationships. Few people, if any, thought it would last with a 16-year age difference, and although it hasn't been easy for us, 10 years later we are still happy and have two beautiful daughters.

- ✔ We grew up in the same neighbourhood with similar family backgrounds but we appear to be very different. In public I am the sociable and impulsive one while

my partner provides the counterbalance of quiet ratio-
nality. We felt a strong bond from our first date and
have been inseparable for over 30 years.

You shouldn't need to do this for more than a couple of
relationships before you realise that when you strip out the
drama from a *real-life* romantic relationship, you end up with
people rubbing along together in a perfectly natural and predictable way.

All human relationships in all walks of life are much like this.
The point is, you know how to do it; you've been doing it all
your life.

Never confuse *romance* with *drama*. Be aware that the destruc-
tive, all-consuming passions and downright bad behaviour of
Scarlett O'Hara and many other tragic, romantic figures are not
what long-term romantic relationships are about.

Realising What Really Matters

In preparation for this chapter, we spoke to many men and
women about what really matters most in a romantic relationship. People have their own preferences, of course, but when
it comes down to the few things that really matter the top
three are:

- **Trust:** Everyone wants to be able to trust and wants to
  be trusted. This doesn't simply mean avoiding cheating
  and barefaced lying. It includes subtler forms of not being
  straightforward such as withholding and avoidance. White
  lies are acceptable to some people and not to others.
  What matters most is that you establish the parameters of
  trust specific to your relationship and stick to them.

- **Communication:** You want to be able to say anything
  you feel the need to say and expect your partner to feel
  the same freedom. In addition, you need to be willing to
  share your important feelings and expect your partner to
  do the same.

Women don't see bottling up things that should be communicated as manly; rather, they see it as a form of withholding or lying.

✔ **Acceptance:** Deep inside, everyone harbours a little neurosis. If you're like most people, you don't quite match up to the image you hold of yourself, so you worry about not being good enough. Couples in all great relationships accept each other, warts and all.

Where are *passion* and *drama* in this list of priorities? It turns out that although most people like a little excitement now and again, intense situations are such a double-edged sword that they don't usually make it onto the must-have list. It's a bit like the farmer's description of New York City: 'nice place to visit; wouldn't want to live there'.

Perhaps a different, lighter form of romantic relating exists – one that can be uplifting and fun but that avoids the deep pitfalls that so often trap the traditional romantic heroes and heroines. If you like the idea of this 'romance-lite', you can build it on the three *must-haves* by adding the following factors:

✔ **A sense of humour:** It may surprise you to know that being funny is sexy, especially when accompanied by self-confidence. Women find a funny, confident man just as irresistible as a drop-dead gorgeous guy. Likewise, men enjoy women who are funny and enjoy a good laugh.

✔ **Thoughtfulness and caring:** A partner who is aware of your needs and takes the trouble to make sure that they're being met is a partner who is reassuring – as long as the care isn't taken to extremes. Good partners are also aware of their own needs and ensure that these needs are being met as well. Being thoughtful goes along with acceptance and includes caring about anything that is important to the loved one, including parents, siblings, and the environment – even the 1957 Cadillac awaiting restoration in the garage.

✔ **The possibility of a compelling future:** This quality is probably the most important of all. The possibility of a compelling future is the true reason that Scarlett couldn't live without her Rhett and its absence probably explains why so many great romantic attachments end in ruins. Belief in a compelling future is the final magical ingredient that makes all the difference. It ensures that you never become bored with each other and never take each other for granted.

Looking at Relationships with Open Eyes

As a human being, you're born into networks of relationships and cannot help accumulating more as you progress through school, jobs, and the expanding relationships your family members and friends embark on. So take on board that you've many relationships already, that being 'in a relationship' is natural to you, and that many, if not most, of your relationships are positive.

Making that first move

What about *the* relationship, though – the relationship with your one true love? What about that one? The stakes do seem a little higher, don't they?

Imagine yourself for a minute on a high wire between two tall buildings. You're crossing to meet your one true love, difficult enough, but in the middle is a fire-breathing dragon of the mediaeval romance kind, and you have to get past it in order to reach your love. As luck would have it, a friendly enchantress advised you in a dream before you set out that you could placate this fiery dragon by repeating a certain magic phrase. Unfortunately, when you woke up you couldn't remember what this magic phrase is. And now here you are, just a short walk from love and fulfilment, facing the probability of certain destruction if you say the wrong thing. How confident do you feel right now? How able are you to take that next step and engage this scary dragon in the make-or-break conversation?

Suddenly you snap to your senses. You're not on a high wire at all; you're at the photocopier standing beside the man or woman of your dreams. Your eyes meet, and in that instant you get a shot at finding that magical, enchanting sentence. You're just as scared, aren't you? Just as certain to end up crashed and burned.

Paradoxically, the person of your dreams is both your love *and* the dragon – what you love the most and what you fear the most. None of it is real in the objective sense; these thoughts are raging around inside your head, swamping your brain with extreme neurochemicals. Do you run away, or do you stay to slay the dragon and earn your prize? This is an old dilemma as Robbie Burns points out in the line: 'faint heart ne're won a lady fair'. Except these days it applies to women too.

So, what can you do? You can prepare; you can guess that you will, sooner or later, be in this position, and you can work out some scenarios. You can work on what is likely to happen. Don't worry if this doesn't sound too romantic, you can work on that later when you're together. This first step is more about survival.

If confidence is about having the power to take the action no matter how you're feeling, then asking for a date is for many people the ultimate test. Everything you've done until now to increase your power and expand your comfort zone comes into play. Your motivation is high, you've thought through all the possible responses, and you realize that no matter what happens, you're unlikely to die from it. There's nothing more to do but jump in!

Fulfilling your partner's needs without running dry yourself

In any mutually dependent relationship, each partner shares the responsibility for each of them getting what they both need. This means that each first has to understand their own needs and then communicate these needs clearly and confidently to their partner.

This arrangement isn't a once-and-for-all limited one like a business contract, but a lifetime commitment to understand and communicate your needs and being sensitive to the developing needs of your partner. How to stay in touch with your own needs and your partner's needs is one of the most important things to know about relationships.

So what happens when one side of the relationship is unable to understand or lacks the confidence to communicate their needs? A lack in this area can damage the relationship to the point of failure and make it impossible to salvage. If you find yourself in this situation, what can you do about it?

ANECDOTE

Dating, the killing fields of confidence

In the western world, *dating* has become the killing fields of the confidence of young men and women. Asking a girl out on a first date is a daunting prospect for a man and if she happens to be the woman of your dreams, it can become paralysing. How do you get yourself to make that move?

You can send your friend to ask her, but this approach is rarely effective much beyond puberty. You can hang around being nice and risk a braver chap stealing your true love if you take too long. The best way, the confident way, is to be authentic and act decisively. But how do you get yourself to pick up the phone or look her straight in the eye and speak out your request?

This challenge is such a universal one for men that Anthony Robbins, the personal power guru, gives a dating lesson on his weekend seminar. The lesson is both brutal and funny to make the point. It culminates in Simon, a wimpish chap from the audience, up on stage asking Sarah, a beautiful, fashionably dressed young woman, to go out for a drink with him. Tough enough, but Robbins has instructed Sarah to refuse vehemently and, each time she is asked again, to pile on the agony even further.

Simon is instructed to keep on asking, regardless of the answer; he is committed to the course of action regardless of the outcome. The result is predictably hilarious and after three or four refusals Sarah is running out of insults. At this point, Simon is beginning to enjoy the game and varies his approach a little, shooting sidelong glances and making gestures to the audience. He is no longer making her refusal mean anything and he is not made wrong or damaged by her response. This is a training drill, of course; in the real world, he could be guilty of harassment as by now he could go on asking her out all night with impunity.

But the amazing thing is that Sarah is also beginning to realise that her refusal has nothing to do with Simon, whom she knows nothing about; she is merely responding to her programming. His refusal to be daunted by the situation is even attractive to her and she becomes a little curious about him despite his ordinary appearance. Simon is no longer just a face chosen at random from the audience but has become an emerging personality and despite the set-up, and the worst imaginable circumstances, a relationship is forming between them. This is life, this is how human beings function, and later Sarah and Simon can be seen chatting about their shared experience over a coffee.

The point of all this is to illustrate how taking committed action and remaining unattached to the outcome is a powerful strategy that can empower you in the most difficult of circumstances. I (Brinley) tried it out on the woman of my dreams as recommended and it took me six months to achieve that first date. It was worth it though, as we are now raising two daughters and will soon be celebrating our fifteenth wedding anniversary.

First, make sure that your partner's need, whatever that need is, doesn't become your need but realise that it creates a new need in you. If your partner is sad or depressed, never try to feel sad and depressed too. You may feel confused, perplexed, and perhaps angry and frustrated that your partner is locking you out by not communicating. Unless you accept your feelings as a natural consequence, you may also come to feel guilty and resentful.

So what do you do? In a serious case, you may want to seek professional counselling or some form of medical intervention, but most situations aren't that serious.

In all cases, stick to the spirit of your responsibility: remain confident, understand your own needs in this situation, and communicate them as honestly as you can. Do your best to explain your feelings in a way that doesn't blame your partner (these are your feelings, and your partner has enough to worry about already), reassure your partner that you're ready and willing to receive their communication whenever he or she is ready, and that you're prepared to help resolve their current problems in whatever way you can, on his or her terms.

That's really about as much as you can do. Monitor your own feelings carefully as they develop. Eventually, your partner may feel more confident and better able to communicate or you may reach a point where you need to seek help. Whatever you do, you can resolve your own feelings most quickly by maintaining full ownership of your end of the problem. These feelings are yours and they derive from your reaction to the current situation. Your response may be based on experiences you had a long time before you met your current partner.

By taking full ownership of your feelings, whatever they are, you are in a more resourceful state from which you can help your partner more confidently.

Getting by with some help from your friends

A good friend or confidant can help you to see your situation more dispassionately than you can alone. If you're having rows and fights with your partner, it may help you to try to step outside the situation and try to see it as a third party may. Remember, every human relationship involves at least two people, two histories, and two sets of strategies – some of which may be helpful and others not.

Be prepared to discover from your current experience, not just what to do for your partner but core facts about yourself: how you operate, what pushes your buttons, and so on. Just because you feel hurt or abused right now doesn't mean that you're always going to feel this way. You can benefit from experiences in your own life and from others. Knowing that you managed to accommodate such problems before or that you know someone who has successfully dealt with a similar situation can build your confidence and give you hope in the darkest times.

Above all, remember that you and your partner are both doing your best at some level. All human interaction is a kind of miracle and building a romantic, long-term relationship is an art that can take a lifetime to perfect.

In a relationship, the journey is much more important than the destination. Like Greek tragedies, even the best romantic relationships are destined to end someday, in death or in life, usually with one partner feeling abandoned and in tears. This is the price you pay for romantic love; if you're smart, you make sure that this price is worth paying by extracting as much joy and fulfilment from your romantic union as possible.

Eliciting Your Love Strategy

How useful would it be to be able to reach out with love to your partner when she or he needs it the most? And how wonderful would it be if your partner had a sure-fire way of making you feel totally loved in those precise moments when you feel alone against the world? You can find out to do this, and doing it isn't that difficult.

You're a creature of habit: you have to be or you'd find it extremely difficult to operate efficiently in this highly complex world. When you find a way to get somewhere, or have a need met, you tend to stick to that method for the rest of your life. You like the same foods at 50 that you liked at 25 (despite complaining they may not like you as much), you often listen to the same styles of music and support the same football teams.

More subtly, you have habitual strategies for doing almost anything, such as deciding what to eat off a menu, getting yourself motivated (or in the mood), even feeling emotions. Strangest of all, you've a time- and experience-honoured method for feeling loved: your *love strategy*.

Allowing yourself to feel loved by another person is an essential ingredient of a romantic relationship, and something you do naturally. But unless you know how you do this, your partner can never achieve it at will, and may feel shut out by you when you're feeling unlovable. And, you may be at your least resourceful when you need reassurance of your 'lovableness' the most.

So how do you find out how you allow yourself to feel loved? Unless you're familiar with the methods of Neuro-linguistic Programming or have participated in a personal development programme on strategy elicitation, you probably haven't a clue. Rest assured, it's an easy thing to work out if you follow some simple steps.

The following steps are easier to run through with an intimate friend or someone else you trust who can work with you to guide you through the stages.

1. **Associate.**

   Eliciting your strategy isn't something you can do in the abstract, so the first thing you need to do is think of a *specific occasion* when you had strong feelings of being loved by someone, it doesn't matter who, and let the memory and its associated feelings flood over you. Let this happen over a few minutes, re-live the moment, and intensify your feelings as far as you're able. When you feel fully associated with that specific time, you're ready for Step 2.

2. **Answer questions.**

   Staying in your associated state, answer the following questions. (This step is easier if you've someone else to ask you the questions and note down your answers.)

   In order for you to feel loved, is it *absolutely necessary* for the other person to show you he or she loves you by:

   • Taking you somewhere? (To your favourite restaurant for example, or a beauty spot?)

- Giving you something? (A personal gift perhaps, or some token chosen with care?)

- Looking at you in some specific way?

- Telling you that you're loved in a certain way (voice tonality, volume, proximity)?

- Touching you in a certain way (place, pressure, duration)? Demonstrate exactly how.

3. Test.

Take your loved one through your answers, and demonstrate exactly how you need to be spoken to, looked at, and touched, and then have your partner speak, look, and touch in the way you describe. Don't be surprised when you melt into feeling totally loved. This is your strategy for feeling love, and you can't help but react in this way.

Knowing the specifics of your own love strategy and helping your partner discover his or hers is enlightening and removes the strong element of chance from this area. If you know how to make a person feel loved by you, you know how to reach out to him or her confidently when he or she needs it the most, and your friends or partner know how to reach out to you.

Facing Relationship Changes

To build a rewarding relationship, you must take on board that you're *always* responsible for what you get from it, no matter what is happening to you. This may seem harsh, even cruel if you're in an abusive relationship, but is the only basis for taking powerful action.

Making decisions

If you're suffering physical or mental abuse, you need to seek help immediately (your abusive partner needs help too, of course, but this responsibility is not yours, nor is it your immediate priority).

If your challenge is less dangerous, though perhaps equally painful as in the case of infidelity, you need to feel your feelings and decide as honestly as you can whether or not you're prepared to work to restore the trust, communication, and acceptance that may have been lost. Be prepared to share all this with your partner and perhaps a professional counsellor. You can never go back to the way things were before, but with work you may arrive at a new and more honest place in your relationship.

In the end, you always get to decide what happens in your life and relationships based on the options you have available. People change, circumstances change, and relationships change too. Change is inherent in living, and is a necessary condition for life. Your free choice is to grow forward confidently into love or to shrink backward into fear. It's your life, and your decision.

Redesigning the way you are together

Whether a troubling situation seems redeemable or irreconcilable, eventually you need to make the decision about re-committing or ending the relationship based on what you feel is best for you. Your partner must do likewise. This includes relationships involving children; you factor them into your judgement about what is best and their wellbeing often motivates you to try as hard as you can to resolve issues as amicably as possible.

If you decide to give the relationship another go, you've the opportunity to enter into a curious state of grace where you can once again consider and redesign as necessary any and all aspects of your relationship together. Leave blame behind at this point – what's done is done. What's more important now is to understand what was lacking in the relationship that allowed the situation to develop. It was probably some of the things on the list in the 'Realising What Really Matters' section earlier in this chapter. Start by looking at whether you've a compelling future and work your way through the other items until you return again to trust. Only by restoring all the elements of a fulfilling relationship can you truly face a better future.

But don't wait for trouble before working on your compelling future. You can start in small ways and not too far out; Rome wasn't built in a day. And remember, a compelling future has to be compelling to both of you. The more you talk and share your inner, deeper desires and longings, the more you have to work with and the more confident you can be in building a life together.

Chapter 15

Connecting Confidently via Social Media

. . . .

In This Chapter

▶ Gaining awareness of social media

▶ Getting up close and personal with social media

▶ Developing your personal and professional social media strategies

▶ Using neurological levels to expand your vision and motivation

. . . .

*I*nteraction with family and friends through online social media services is a way for individuals to engage and stay engaged with people they value, wherever they are. As market-leading services like Facebook and Twitter have become widely and freely available, they've been massively adopted by users the world over as a valuable addition to their lives. But while millions of people love social media, nearly as many are wary of and even fear it.

Social media services are also gaining popularity in the workplace, with professionals using the online profiling and communication tools for interacting with colleagues and customers and for managing their careers. Many people find professional use of social media more challenging, and lack the confidence to publish their profiles, qualifications, and ambitions openly online. They're uncertain and question the wisdom of openly connecting with business contacts in this way. Social media is making them reappraise the wisdom of their previous private use of the media as they hear scare stories about online scams, identity theft and online gaffes that have damaged people's reputations and finances.

A fully engaged social and professional person in the early years of the 21st century needs to be able to use social media powerfully and confidently. To do that successfully takes a little time; time to build your networks and your online reputation. So, in this chapter, we expand your understanding of social media, explain how engaging with it in all aspects of your life can be a positive and powerful move for you, and outline the best ways to engage fully, professionally, and confidently.

Social media is developing fast, so anything we write about specific products and their capabilities becomes outdated quickly. For this reason, we look at today's market-leading services only. For a more detailed and up-to-date summary, take a look at other *For Dummies* titles (such as *Facebook For Dummies* by Leah Pearlman and Carolyn Abram, *LinkedIn For Dummies* by Joel Elad, *Twitter For Dummies* by Laura Fitton, Michael Gruen and Leslie Poston, and *YouTube For Dummies* by Doug Sahlin and Chris Botello (all published by Wiley) dedicated to major social media services and search the Internet for the latest developments.

Harnessing the Collective Power

Simply, *social media* is the collective term for public services you use to interact with people electronically. These services are simple to pick up and easy to use. In terms of interaction, using social media is no different from speaking with someone on the phone or sending email, but social media has other powerful properties for interaction, depending on the service you're using:

- ✔ **Connect with other people:** You can set up online communication channels, where you *connect* or *link* to your friends, professional colleagues and business contacts. Then, when you want to say something to them, these links are already in place for you to use.

- ✔ **Keep up with your contacts:** You can receive automatic notifications about your contacts, such as when they change their status, when they post a message or a picture, and when they update their curriculum vitae (CV) or change job. They don't have to remember to tell you directly.

- ✔ **Send messages:** You can send messages to a single person or to thousands of people at the same time (though you'd be quickly overwhelmed if many of them decided to reply).

✓ **Follow other people:** You can elect to receive status messages from hundreds of people (including world-famous people like film or music stars), and get regular updates and notifications from them.

✓ **Share photos and videos:** You can transmit and exchange photos and video footage via services like YouTube. And you can broadcast to thousands or even millions of people at the same time.

✓ **Post updates:** You can post updates of your own on free website space that's dedicated to your personal use on a private or public 'wall' or notice board that other people can reply to if they want. (You don't have to address these messages to anyone in particular, and you can limit who sees your notices to specific friends and colleagues.)

Interacting through social media is like being unbounded in space and time. You can interact instantly with anyone who has an Internet connection, anywhere on Earth, at any time of day, seven days a week. Your Internet friends can massively outnumber your regular friends and you can be more up-to-date and know more about their lives.

Working out what the attraction is

Social media usage is on the rise. In the five years between the first edition and this edition of *Confidence For Dummies*, the number of users on Facebook alone has increased almost ten-fold. However, relatively few of those people, as yet, have fully engaged with social media in all its powerful aspects. Most people remain a little wary of it, and lack the confidence to do this.

Social media has detractors as well as fans. Whereas many millions of people of all ages spend more time on social media websites than they spend watching TV, many others are concerned about privacy and security issues and, frankly, they don't see the attraction.

Whichever camp you're in today, you probably have many family members, friends and professional colleagues who are spending increasing amounts of time online connecting and interacting with other friends and colleagues. It may not be long before you feel as if you're missing out, not only on what your children and friends are up to, but because your professional colleagues are having important debates online that you aren't showing up to.

Social media is increasingly not just social; it's everywhere, and it's powerful. Your ability to communicate freely and easily with other people and with the businesses whose products and services you consume is changing the traditional game of consumer marketing and service provision. Similarly, the ability of workers to share their experience of specific employers with fellow professionals is changing the willingness of organisations to understand and engage with their workforces. And even politicians and media figures realise that they're under greater scrutiny with faster public retribution than ever before.

Social media really is a communications revolution, one that you need to come to terms with and discover how to use in all parts of your life as confidently and powerfully as you currently use your more traditional ways of engaging with people.

Using the most popular services

Competing social media services abound and they all have different strengths and features. The following sections focus on four of the most popular and well-known services.

Hooking up on Facebook

Facebook is currently the biggest social media service and is fast approaching an incredible billion registered users. If Facebook were a country, it would have the third-biggest population in the world, behind China and India, and it may grow bigger than both of them combined in a few years.

Most of the billion people registered to use Facebook began by using its features to stay in touch with close family and friends. This use remains Facebook's primary one, although it is branching out into many other features and services thanks to the incredible popularity of the service.

Facebook is a brilliantly simple idea. Register with the service and you're given a *wall* upon which you can post pieces of information and news, invitations, acknowledgements, photos and whatever else you may want to post up, a bit like a communal pin board. Your *friends* (people you've agreed to link with through Facebook) can see your postings and add comments as they wish. In return, you can see their walls and post comments or reply to their comments in the same way.

These casual activities are all that the majority of Facebook users do, but a more serious side to Facebook exists, which is growing rapidly too. This side is its use in business for profiling, understanding and predicting consumer behaviour and promoting business and services.

Linking in

LinkedIn is currently the leading professional social media site, and has over 150 million members. It's a networking site, where you've a profile that's a bit like a CV that you keep up to date.

LinkedIn works on the six degrees of separation principle (see the nearby sidebar on this topic), which helps you to connect more effectively with your extended network. As we write, Brinley's 650 direct contacts can immediately introduce him to 6.5 million other fellow professionals, and still it grows: the software proudly tells Brinley that a further 19,000 people have showed up in his extended network in the last 72 hours.

~~Six~~ Four degrees of separation

Six degrees of separation refers to the idea that no one is more than six introductions away, on average, from any other person on Earth. This statement means that a short chain of 'a friend of a friend' introductions can connect any two people on the planet. The Hungarian author Frigyes Karinthy originally came up with the idea back in the 1920s. Karinthy had the insight that the world was becoming a smaller place thanks to the ways humans were increasingly connected. In spite of the great physical distances between people on different sides of the world, the growing density of human networks made the actual social distance far smaller.

No doubt Karinthy would have been a fan of Facebook. The University of Milan has analysed 69 billion connections on the service and announced that each person is now separated by an average of only four links to everyone else on the site, including the Queen of England and the president of the United States.

The kind of rapid networking that LinkedIn affords is valuable to many professionals. People unknown to you (especially search consultants, recruiters and prospective customers) can immediately see your growing professional profile, and get in touch. Before you know it, your knowledge, career and ultimately your confidence are all receiving a welcome boost. If you aren't fully profiled on LinkedIn yet, ask yourself why not? You're missing out.

Tweeting

Twitter is second only to Facebook in the growing range of massively adopted social media products. It's a social media service that instantly sends messages of 140 characters or less to people who have signed up specifically to receive these short messages from you.

And so you know what 140 characters looks like, this short paragraph is precisely 140 characters long, if you include the punctuation marks.

The Twitter founders came up with the 140 character limit to emulate the maximum length of a standard phone text message or SMS. And in the world of smart phones, Twitter has become SMS with the addition of powerful broadcast features.

Twitter launched in July 2006. By autumn 2011, it had grown to over 200 million users who were broadcasting almost 200 million tweets every day. Celebrity advocates of Twitter are hooked – sending out huge numbers of tweets every day to promote their image, their lifestyles, their thoughts and actions.

Twitter also has a growing business side, which has proven itself to be a uniquely powerful medium for the instant dissemination of information to people who need and value it.

Blogging

All sorts of platforms allow you to blog. Popular services are Google's Blogger and WordPress. A *blog*, or *web log* to give it its original name, is a website or part of a website where people regularly post information, a bit like an online diary. Often, people reading the blog can post comments and subscribe to the blog's *feed*, which sends them updates each time new content appears.

Over 150 million blogs of various types – personal, corporate, media, political and cultural – are currently available to anyone who wants to read them.

 Most quality journalism is now available through blogs, which readers can sign up to follow alongside or instead of their daily newspaper. The blog is often more current and detailed than its equivalent news story or commentary.

Getting to Grips with the Basics When You're a Newbie

When you first see someone's Facebook page, it looks like a free-for-all with folk engaged in a mad banter of trivia, well-wishing, flirting, gossiping and announcing their news, accompanied by crazy photographs. It looks like a written-down version of lunchtime in a school: noisy, funny, largely well-meaning and slightly competitive, and you may feel uncertain how to navigate your way through it all. Don't worry – in this section we get you social-media-ready, to the point where you feel you can behave with confidence in a social media environment.

Getting stuck in

Although the benefits of social media are so broad and generally available to anyone free of charge, you may still be reluctant to get involved beyond the occasional use of Facebook. Many people are. This is a question of confidence: you need to see the big picture and understand the benefits of engaging online so you don't feel the need to push through your anxieties to get to grips with it.

The strong commercial, technological, personal and professional forces at work within social media are creating a kind of perfect storm that won't go away and can't be ignored. We believe that you're certain to get more involved at some stage, so why not face your fears and take the plunge now; making social media work for you can boost your confidence mission to live life powerfully in all its parts.

Taking your time to get comfortable with social media

If you're completely new to social media, ask your friends to help you take a closer look at their online conversations. You can see quickly that people engage in subtly different ways. Some people are loud, others are quieter; some appear extrovert and others are modest. In short, social media is like a large crowd of people doing what they do; each has his circle of friends who presumably like to relate in the way that he does.

Comfort is a key factor here. You need to feel comfortable as you develop understanding and skills. For example, one of the miracles of social media is that no two people see exactly the same pages. You can set privacy controls about who sees your messages and your photos. You choose whether to limit this access to your good friends and family members, or extend it to a wider circle as you see fit.

On social media everyone does their own thing. Don't feel any pressure to imitate anyone, do anything or disclose anything you feel uncomfortable about. You can start by just watching or reading, rather than fully interacting. Take it slowly and extend your engagement only when you want to, as you become more familiar with the features of the different services and how you use them. Choose one service at a time (most people start with Facebook) and move on to trying others only when you're comfortable with how it works.

Getting help to engage

Some people coming to social media for the first time may never have used a personal computer before. If you're in this position, or have friends or family who are, be very patient. Other people come to social media via smartphones and other consumer devices, which are generally easier to use, when you understand the basics. Even so, you need to set up your contacts and connections carefully, first finding them and then ensuring that you treat your friends as friends and colleagues as colleagues, online as you would do in person.

Social media services are aimed at the mass consumer audience, so they're easy to pick up and they work the way you expect them to work, which isn't always the case with other kinds of software you may have had bad experiences with. But getting started safely on social media can seem complicated. Our advice is to find an experienced friend or professional adviser to help you. In many families, younger members have experience enough to get you up and running. Trust them; they often enjoy being 'in the know' and can give you good advice on how to manage your contacts and maintain privacy (whether or not they follow this advice themselves).

As social media becomes more complex, the options you have around who can see what and how you can categorise your friends are increasing. For this reason, speak to someone who understands or find a recent article on a website that advises you exactly how to set up your privacy preferences.

Benefitting From a Social Media Strategy

Against the background of the explosive growth of social media and growing awareness of the risks, it's unsurprising that many people remain uncertain and reluctant to engage fully. By forming a social media strategy, though, you can create a positive and confident way of achieving your objectives. Most people find social media to be an efficient, convenient and fun way of staying in touch with friends and family from a distance. In this case, your objective is staying in touch at a distance while having fun. Your *strategy* is how you plan to achieve this objective most efficiently.

Forming your basic approach

You may not realise it, but you already have some kind of plan for staying in touch, even if it just resides at the back of your mind. For example, you've different kinds of social interactions with your family (old and young), close friends, old friends, friends of friends, and so on, and you won't always want them to know exactly the same information about you. Staying in touch with these different groups through social media is more complicated than it may at first appear if you want to do it well, though, as Facebook and other services have yet to give you the power to 'segment' your audiences so that you can be confident about sending them different messages.

Most people deal with this problem through compromising their behaviour. On Facebook, for example, they take care not to be too outrageous with their messages, even to friends, knowing that younger family members may also be reading them. But if you've friends who can be thoughtless and indiscrete, you may want to manage what they say or control the pictures they post.

In truth, you can't always manage other people, so you might want to take care not to connect with relatives who might be shocked by the odd indiscretion (like parents or children depending on your age). Likewise, you may prefer to exclude professional contacts (your boss, clients and other people) in front of whom you'd be embarrassed. And then hope that nothing too bad about you emerges.

Compromising your behaviour, hoping for the best, and ignoring anything you don't like hardly makes for a confident personal social media strategy but, at best, it remains fairly efficient as a strategy for staying in touch at a distance. The cost, of course, is that you exclude certain people and certain information.

A more effective strategy is to use Facebook only for family and friends and to limit your social interaction in business to LinkedIn. This strategy works fairly well for many people, but is under threat as more and more business contacts are showing up in Facebook networks, so you need to remain careful.

In addition to social interaction in business, social media is fast growing as a vital tool of engagement for business professionals of all kinds, to the extent that not engaging is a threat to your own future success at work. As the leading social media services have quickly gained a billion enthusiastic users worldwide, something new has come into being: people all over the world becoming connected at an unprecedented rate by giant networks of mind-boggling scale. And as hundreds of millions of individuals use functions such as the 'like' button to endorse opinions, websites and products, they create a social network of enormous value to the business world.

Because of these effects, social media has become a competitive battleground for businesses, who are discovering how to use it to engage with their customers, to manage their brand reputations and to understand their customers' needs. How well businesses do these things is fast becoming a big influence on their success, and they need people-connecting skills and values at all levels in their workforce. To play your part in these developments, you need to be confident in using social media.

Although effective personal social media strategy and best practices and policies are yet to fully emerge, do keep thinking about them and about the specific areas where you must work hard to be effective: protecting your privacy and security.

Considering your online privacy

When thinking about your social media strategy, two aspects need your special attention right from the start and across all areas: your personal online privacy and security.

If you've ever seen a photo of yourself looking silly or worse, taken when you weren't expecting it – at a party, say, or on holiday – you may have felt a wave of embarrassment and urged your friends to move on quickly to the next picture in the pack. Now imagine that same picture posted online, available for anyone to see, copy and re-post forever, with little redress. This eventuality can and does happen every day on social media services, so it's no wonder people get anxious about protecting their privacy online.

As a strategy for dealing with this problem, many people try to 'police' their privacy by asking friends to cooperate and by separating their social and professional social media interactions – sharing a degree of privacy in social areas, such as Facebook, and focusing strictly on professional aspects in a service like LinkedIn. But unless you proactively manage your entire online profile, you won't even know what's out there.

 Anyone searching for you online can usually locate references to your personal life. And if you give your online profile no consideration, the most prominent thing about you on the web may well be something you don't want the whole world to know. The only solution to this problem is not to try to hide your online presence but to create and manage a fuller online identity with more positive stories.

As well as thinking about what you actively share online, become familiar with privacy settings on all the services you're signed up for. These settings get changed occasionally by the service provider so you need to remain alert to what you're showing to whom.

Considering your online security

Most people can live with the pressure of an embarrassing but innocent photograph of themselves showing up on someone else's Facebook wall, but another level of threats to your online security exists. As in other walks of life, a small proportion of people in the social media world are not what they pretend to be. Sadly, because the numbers of people engaging in social media are so huge, they're attractive to organised crime, which represents a sizable threat. The two threats that most people are aware of and most fear are fraud and identity theft.

In criminal law, a *fraud* or *scam* is an intentional deception made for personal gain or to damage another individual, and criminals seek to do this online in various ways. An *advance-fee fraud*, for example, is a confidence trick in which someone persuades you to advance money in the hope of realising a significantly larger gain. Common examples include the Nigerian letter scam, the Spanish prisoner, the black money scam and the Russian/Ukrainian and romance scams. You can find out more about these frauds and their variants online.

You can easily protect yourself from the vast majority of these fraudsters by using common sense and maintaining high online ethical standards. If anything looks suspicious or shady, err on the side of caution and treat it as though it is suspicious or shady. If anyone offers you a deal that looks too good to be true, then it probably is. If anyone asks you to do something unethical, even if it seems to be in a good cause, don't touch it.

Here are some other don'ts to build into your social media strategy to protect your privacy and security:

- ✔ Never share your date of birth unnecessarily. This key piece of information gets asked for in legitimate security questions that protect you against fraudulent activity on your finances, so if fraudsters have it, it no longer works in your favour.

- ✔ Never mention in your online status updates that you're off on holiday for a fortnight. You're effectively announcing that your home is empty and vulnerable.

✔ Never denounce an unpopular policy at your place of work or reveal confidential information about a colleague. You may be liable to disciplinary action and dismissal.

Generating a professional social media strategy

Defining an effective social media strategy is easier in business, where the rules are so much clearer, than in your private life. In business, a lack of clear strategy and control would be a critical issue, and anything that appears like a slapdash personal approach can quickly land you in trouble. You can get fired, end up in court, go out of business, and even go to prison if you get it badly wrong. In business, you need a rigorous social media strategy and a set of rules (or *policies*) for maintaining better control.

For these reasons, some businesses have extremely restrictive social media policies, and even lock people out of the major social media sites. This limited short-term thinking is likely to change but, in the meantime, the world won't stop to wait for laggards. If you run your own business, you need a more confident and better-informed approach.

Staying aware

For generations, the traditional approach to business in consumer societies has been to understand what consumers want and then to convince them that what you're offering is an appropriate and cost-effective way of them meeting that want. This is why using social media as a tool for finding out what your customers and competitors are thinking and saying to each other is marketing gold dust; and a whole new army of analysts and advisors has quickly grown up to help you to hear and understand what is going on.

Inconveniently, though, the online conversations you need to engage with in business don't all say complimentary things about your products and services, so you must have the ability and confidence to engage effectively in the most difficult of conversations, with unhappy and sometimes unreasonable customers, in public!

This situation is new and extremely discomforting for traditional business thinking, which relies on poor communication between customers to buy time to rectify problems and convince people that a bad experience is a rare and unfortunate occurrence.

Just a few years ago, for example, if you bought a book from a surly shop assistant and didn't enjoy reading it, that was your problem. Then online retailers came along and gave customers the means and the freedom to tell the world just what they thought, including that the retailer's delivery was poor and the book was bad, if that was their experience. Now every customer has the ability read these comments and join in the free-for-all if they want to. They don't even need your website to do this; they can equally do it on social media services like Twitter, and you cannot prevent it. But you need to at least know about it and, increasingly, you must engage with it.

This, and other changes in the way online retailers and modern businesses are finding out how to respect and treat their customers, are setting a blistering pace for more traditionally minded businessmen and women. But there's no going back. People, especially children, are being shaped and educated by their social media experience in this way, and everyone needs to pick up the new rules quickly, no matter how uncomfortable they make you feel.

Committing to engagement

Whether you work for yourself or for a company, you need to make sure that you and your colleagues are committed to a long-term social engagement with your clients, suppliers and partners through the two-way street of social media. When you've a commitment to engage, use this process to establish and execute your strategy:

1. **Set out the objectives you hope to achieve by using social media (things like increasing brand recognition, growing positive sentiment, increasing your network of relationships and boosting traffic to your website).**

   These objectives need to be SMART (we set out how to set SMART objectives in Chapter 3) as you are going to measure your progress against them.

2. **Do your research.**

Start by searching online for your own business, brands and products, and create a list of the sites where they show up. These sites are those where you can immediately engage with people in your target zone. In addition to the giants of Facebook, LinkedIn and Twitter, search for niche blogs and forums specific to your industry. You can also search for references to your competitors to find other places to engage.

3. **Read the blogs and monitor the key issues and people on these sites.**

The online world has leaders and influencers and certain sites become magnets for new ideas. When you're ready to engage, start posting comments and responses to join in the conversations. Raise your own questions and suggestions for people to respond to – an excellent way to test out your thinking and ideas to get early feedback.

4. **Analyse your results.**

Measure and analyse your social media activity against your SMART goals to squeeze out every last drop of insight and intelligence you can glean from your experience. Use your findings to adapt and finesse the next stages of your tactical execution.

By following these four simple steps, you're far better able to thread your way successfully through the clamour and chaos of social media marketing. And remember, social media are meant to supplement and enrich normal human relationships, not replace them. Continue to meet people 'in the flesh' whenever you can to pursue more conventional marketing and business development.

Things don't tend to happen instantly. For social media to work for you in business, you need to be part of the community, which means that you need to show up consistently. You don't need to spend hours and hours each day on Twitter, Facebook or LinkedIn, but you do need to be there regularly, as you would in any other relationship.

Connecting Yourself to the Bigger Network

Whatever your level of engagement is with social media, with sufficient confidence you can almost certainly increase it to achieve greater personal and business benefit.

A powerful starting point from which to give your social media activity a boost is to use the neurological levels framework that we introduce in Chapter 7. First consider each of the levels – environment, behaviour, capabilities, beliefs, identity, and beyond – from the bottom up (allowing you to smooth out inconsistencies and ensure that your behaviours and capabilities support your values). Now you can see where you've been holding back online and playing a smaller game than you could. By repeating the exercise from the top down, you can increase your aspiration at each level and create a more inspirational vision of the fully connected person you can be.

If you've completed the self-structure exercise we describe in Chapter 7, you already have a powerful and congruent vision of your bigger self in the world. You know what's most important to you, you've a set of beliefs that empower you, you know the capabilities you need and, above all, you've defined your chosen mission in life (for the foreseeable future anyway).

Now you're ready to really get connected – confidently. Social media provides you with a powerful way to extend your reach and influence in the world, to stay grounded and connected to your loved ones while reaching out to the bigger world beyond.

Part V
The Part of Tens

The 5th Wave   By Rich Tennant

ATTEMPTING TO REDUCE THE ANXIETY IN HIS LIFE, WALDO "WHIP" GUNSCHOTT GOES FROM BEING A WILD ANIMAL TRAINER, TO A WILD BALLOON ANIMAL TRAINER.

In this part . . .

Stop by here whenever you want a quick fix of confidence inspiration. These chapters offer a set of questions to ask yourself when you need to get up and going, plus great reminders of what you can do on a daily basis to build your confidence.

Chapter 16

Ten Great Questions to Spur You into Action

Confidence is about taking the action to realise your dreams. The questions that follow are meant to get you up and out there, being your most confident self.

How Does Your Inner Voice Speak to You?

An inner dialogue goes on inside you all the time. Even as you read this question, you may be asking yourself: 'What does this mean? How does my voice speak to me?' Your inner voice tries to make sense of the question.

What kind of voice do you have inside – a nurturing and pleasant one, or a miserable and grumpy critic who's too hard to please? Do you hear: 'Well done, me. That was a good conversation I had there. Things are going well and I'm on track.' Or is it more: 'There I go again, putting my foot in it, what a silly oaf. What did I do that for? I'll never be any good at this, will I?'

Remember that the quality of your thoughts dictates the quality of your confident action. So, start tuning into the inner dialogue in your head. If you hear it running you down and being highly critical, practice replying with some positive phrases like: 'I did my best there' or 'I can improve from this' or even 'Hey ho, it's time to let that one go.' If you look after yourself from the inside in this way, you're on track for confident action on the outside.

Are You Proud of Your Name?

Have you ever received a call that goes like this: 'Sorry to bother you, but . . . I've been asked to talk to you about X, Y, Z.' When no name is used, no sense of identity occurs.

Always lead with your name before you state your business: 'Hello, I'm . . . and I'd like to talk to you about X, Y, Z.' Volunteer your name, look directly at the person, and state your name with a smile whenever you introduce yourself. Even when you're speaking on the phone and can't see the other person, stay smiling and imagining their face, and the energy will come through – you really can 'hear' a smile over the telephone.

When you're proud of who you are, other people value you more. Set the expectation that you're a person of worth and valuable to connect with.

Who Do You Hang Out With?

Choose your friends wisely. Do the people you spend time with pull you up or push you down? Fire 'toxic' friends – those who drain your energy and enthusiasm, leaving you wilting and exhausted and, in their place, find people who are good role models for you – people who demonstrate a quality that you'd like more of. Discover all you can about how they got to where they are. Tap into their sense of confidence and share it – they have plenty to go round. When you find someone who has conquered the fears you want to let go of, use them as a role model of success.

What's Your Confident Thought for the Day?

For many years now, the British BBC Radio 4 *Today* programme has offered a 'Thought for the Day' slot. During this three-minute slot, unedited by the programme's producers, an eminent thinker or theologian has the chance to air their words of wisdom. The speakers pose moral questions to the listener on a theme that links to a topical item in current affairs.

Now comes your turn. Imagine you have a three-minute slot on the radio to give your confident thought for the day. If you had a chance to share your wisdom with the nation on how it should act with confidence, what would your message be? Notice that when you can come up with your own suggestions, you have insights and wisdom that other people can benefit from. By standing in the spotlight in this way, articulating your ideas, you can boost your own confidence.

Where Are the Tensions in Your Life?

Every day you make choices and decisions on how to spend your time. You say 'yes' to some things and 'no' to others. All of this creates fundamental tension, balancing, and getting the balance adjusted in the best way for you. You may be juggling challenges such as:

- **Your health versus your wealth:** Perhaps you're working hard to earn money, but that's not leaving you time to look after your health.

- **Your family and work life:** Perhaps family commitments are preventing you from doing the kind of work you want, or you have a job where you're travelling and not able to be with your family as much as you wish.

✔ **Time for yourself and time for other people:** Maybe you spend so much time looking after other people that you have no time for yourself, or vice versa.

✔ **Spontaneity today or planning for tomorrow:** You want to enjoy the moment and also plan for the future.

Look at the tensions you face up to every day in your life. By exploring the pluses and minuses you face, you can then ask yourself: 'What is the right answer – even if it's not easy to carry out?' Make changes so that you go with what you consider is *right* rather than what you feel is the *easiest* option. Chapter 5 helps you identify your core values.

What's Your Sticking Point?

One area in your life may keep cropping up as something to sort out, but you never quite get round to it. You know that you need to, and yet nothing changes. Maybe you need to make time to nurture a significant relationship, to get your weight to a healthy figure on the scales, or your bank balance or home in order.

Allow yourself to uncover all the positive benefits you'll enjoy when you've cracked this one. Consider all the other areas in your life where you'll feel happier and more confident as a result. After you crack this one, you'll release energy for other things in your life to take off.

It may be that you need to overcome procrastination or that you haven't made it your top priority. Chapter 8 offers practical advice to break through these barriers, regardless of how difficult the task or how little time you have. Changing one small habit or taking one step forward can make all the difference.

Who Are You Going to Be When You Grow Up?

When you were young, you may have had thoughts of who you were going to be when you grew up. Most people don't manage to make it as a ballet dancer, film star, or astronaut. Today you may have a more regular kind of job or life – a builder, a banker, or a bakery assistant. By facing reality and responsibility, you stop considering who you are and what you can become. You may be selling yourself short and limiting yourself by a lack of imagination and willingness to be open to new possibilities.

Allow yourself to consider who you really want to be for a while, and notice as you do so what symbol or image comes to you. Holding that symbol in front of you, follow it and see where it leads you. When you've identified who you really want to be, you can start to figure out the first steps you need to take to get there. (Turn to Chapter 13 for tips on discovering your life's work.)

How Do You Experience Failures and Mistakes?

Confident people regard failures and mistakes as necessary stepping stones on the journey through life. Rejection is just another hoop to get through on the way onward and upward. Like the character of Tigger in the Winnie the Pooh stories, these people bounce back for more whenever they get brushed off.

As great inventors and scientists know, success takes persistence. Each time an experiment doesn't work out, they take another look at the painstaking records of every detail of their experiments, make adjustments, and try again.

To be a winner you need tough skin, and you succeed by viewing failure as a temporary inconvenience and a step in the direction of achieving your goals. So, after any rejection, take stock and remind yourself of your VAT factor – V is for *Values*, the things important to you that help guide your choices and decisions; A is for *Aims*, your goals, the things you want to achieve, and T is for *Talents*, all those qualities of excellence you have. (Chapter 13 has a section on dealing with rejection confidently.)

How Do You Balance Time Alone and Time with Others?

A mark of a confident person is that they're at ease in the company of other people, and equally content with their own company. In particular, they can spend time alone without constantly seeking to have people buzzing around them. Time alone is necessary to replenish your sense of calmness, centring, and comfort in being your naturally confident self.

If you feel that your confidence is waning, check that you've had space for yourself to regain your personal balance, and that you're not feeling overwhelmed with the demands and distractions of being with other people. Get centred in order to take effective action.

What's Your 120 Per Cent Dream?

How often do you allow yourself to dream about what your life can really, really be like? What kind of project or exploration would shift your life to an extraordinary one? Did you have ambitious dreams for yourself when you were young and then life got in the way? So what about having a 120 per cent dream – a dream beyond the dream, something that's so exciting and so enticing that you can't fail to want it and move towards it?

Make it a big dream, a goal that really motivates you. Write it down in as much detail as you can, really getting into how it will look and feel when you achieve it. Every day go and review it and take one action, implement one daily habit, however tiny, that takes you closer to your 120 per cent dream. At the same time, let go of one negative action or thought that gets in the way of your success. (Chapter 12 provides practical guidance to get the results you want.)

Chapter 17

Ten Daily Habits to Raise Your Confidence

● ●

In This Chapter

▶ Finding easy ways to build your confidence muscles

▶ Starting your day in the best way

▶ Getting in tune with yourself

▶ Working out what's best for you

● ●

*B*uilding your confidence doesn't happen overnight; confidence building is more of a drip-feed activity that starts with every day actions. Habits have a way of repeating themselves, so get into good habits and you're off to a flying start.

Start Each Day Alert and Ready for Action

'Early to bed and early to rise, makes a man healthy, wealthy, and wise' according to Benjamin Franklin. You've 168 hours in a week, and you're likely to spend about a third of those hours in bed. How you create the quality of the remaining two-thirds of each day is up to you.

Do you ever have those days when the alarm goes off, you put it on the snooze feature, it goes off again, and again, and you eventually turn it off or hide it under the pillow? How does your day pan out when you get up late and head out of the door in a manic rush? Just notice, though, what happens when you have a calm and relaxed start to the day, when you get out of bed at a reasonable hour and then take things in your stride.

Confident people love life so much that they don't want to waste a minute of it. Start your day 'on the front foot' – that is, ready and prepared to proactively engage with the day, and you won't waste the rest of it trying to catch up with yourself.

Concentrate Your Mind on the Page

Studies in the workplace show that it takes up to 15 minutes to get your concentration back after a phone call. Just a few interruptions and your day drifts aimlessly away. You may not be a Zen meditator, but any drill that trains you to stop your thoughts wandering and to arrive in the 'here and now' pays dividends. (*Mindfulness For Dummies* by Shamash Alidina (Wiley) is a great resource to dip into here.)

Writing pages is a useful concentration habit to develop. Take three sides of paper – A4 size or smaller if you prefer. Write whatever comes into your head. Don't worry about there being a right or wrong way to write, you don't need to feel inspired by great creative verses. Just write anything – strictly stream-of-consciousness stuff: 'Hello blank pages, I haven't a clue what to write, but I'm writing anyway.' Continue until you've filled the pages. Then, as if by magic, something useful emerges from the page. Some people write such pages every day; others write them as and when they feel the need.

The discipline of writing your thoughts on a blank page acts as an invaluable brain dump in the morning to quieten the busy and logical part of your mind and get you centred and creative.

Put Your Best Sunglasses On

Imagine if you'd got up this morning and put on a pair of rose-coloured sunglasses. You'd be travelling through your day armed with a warm, healthy glow. Everybody and everything you see would take on a pinky hue. In a way, every day you do put on a pair of sunglasses. They act as a filter through which you perceive the world. You may just not be aware of what type of filter you've chosen.

By consciously choosing your sunglasses for the day, you decide how to frame your experiences that day. You decide whether the day is going to be rich and precious, full of interesting experiences, or one of constant battles to be fought. Your experience begins in your own head. As you start each day, decide which sort of glasses you're wearing.

Here are some examples to try on for size: My glasses for today are . . . savour each moment to the full . . . look for the best in the situation . . . find the humour in unlikely situations and people . . . enjoy the sounds/aromas/tastes around me.

Track Your Moods and Emotions

How are you today emotionally? Do you know how you feel and how you feel it? Emotionally intelligent people have a high level of awareness – they stay in tune with how they're feeling and the effect they have on other people.

Do a stock check during the day and begin to notice what's going on inside you. When do you feel confident and when not? How do you know what you're feeling – what are the telltale signals in your body? How do other people around you know what you're thinking – is it written on your face or conveyed by the tone of your voice or your behaviour? By tracking your moods, you've a measure of where you're at in case you need to refine the direction. (Chapter 6 shows you how to make friends with your emotions.)

Exercise Your Body

Strange as it seems, you can go to the gym feeling tired, exercise, and come away feeling energised. Your brain loves exercise. In the past few years, researchers have contradicted the commonly held belief that you're born with a fixed number of neurons and produce no more during your lifetime. Even adults can grow new brain cells, and exercise is one of the best ways to achieve this growth.

The good news is that exercise doesn't have to be too vigorous. Just walking sedately for half an hour a day improves your scores on abilities such as learning, concentration, and abstract reasoning. Senior citizens who walk regularly perform better on memory tests than their counterparts who sit around more. Likewise researchers have found that schoolchildren aged 10 and 11 who exercise three or four times a week get higher than average exam grades.

Find a form of exercise that you enjoy and do it regularly. (Chapter 10 offers more tips on developing your physical confidence.)

Take Quiet Moments Alone

How are you with the power of silence? If you're used to rushing around and being with people non-stop, then taking ten minutes to sit quietly alone may be an enlightening experience.

So try the following every single day: switch off your phone, your door bell, your computer, your TV, and your radio. Go to a place where no one and nothing can disturb you. Sit there quietly without talking or interruption for ten minutes. Allow yourself to dream while you're free of internal chatter and noise. Just empty your mind, experience the space, and let your creativity unfold.

Go Outside and Wonder at the Beauty of the Sky

Remember, a whole world lies outside your door. Take time each day to get out there and stop to notice the natural world, the passing of the seasons, and the changing patterns in the sky.

Notice how you're part of something so much bigger than you and your immediate environment, and enjoy the beauty of it all. Even if you live in a big city, it's free and fun to go barefoot in the park.

Operate from a Position of Generosity

What goes round comes round. Whatever you give out has a habit of coming back to you in some way or another. Confident people act from a position of generosity and abundance. They give what they can, when they can – whether their time, talent, money, energy, or love.

Aim to give to others and remember to give to yourself too. Generous thoughts nurture your mind and attract generous people to you.

Review Today and Create Your Tomorrow

At the end of each day, mentally review what happened and how you experienced it. Perhaps the day worked out pretty much as planned but you didn't get as much done as you thought you would. You can benefit from your experience; perhaps you habitually give yourself too much to do.

Every night before you turn out the light, write down the five most important things you want to do tomorrow. They can be anything at all, but make sure that they're the important things and the ones that fit with your values. While you sleep, your unconscious mind is working out for you how you can achieve them most easily.

In the morning, before you get out of bed, take your list and decide how to fit the tasks and activities into your day. If it looks a tight fit, start with the most important and leave out the least important.

You now have a day's schedule that should ensure that you stay focused.

Connect with Your Life Purpose

If you were to ask yourself right now 'Why am I alive? What's my life about?' you may not have an instant answer. With a little probing, you'd soon arrive at something along the lines of: 'I want to make a difference. I want to make the world a better place. I want to create love, joy, magic, harmony, peace, and so on. I want to be an example to others. I want to live a good life.' (Chapter 5 guides you toward uncovering your values.)

Your confident action is based on the meaning you make of what happens for you day by day, year by year. This meaning is why the way you experience confidence is so different from the person next to you. No one can give you the magic confidence pill to take and make everything wonderful for you. You need to find the confidence for yourself.

As you accept that you're responsible for your own journey, you find more clarity and freedom, and thus the confidence to be yourself and do what is right for you. As you travel through each day, hold the bigger picture of your life and make sure that what you're doing now fits well with the bigger picture. Then you can simply enjoy being alive, knowing that you're being your most confident self.

Index

FOR DUMMIES®

Making Everything Easier! ™

UK editions

SINESS

Bookkeeping
FOR DUMMIES

978-0-470-97626-5

Persuasion & Influence
FOR DUMMIES

978-0-470-74737-7

Starting & Running a Business
ALL-IN-ONE
FOR DUMMIES

978-1-119-97527-4

FERENCE

British Politics
FOR DUMMIES

978-0-470-68637-9

DIY
FOR DUMMIES

978-0-470-97450-6

Dad's Guide to Pregnancy
FOR DUMMIES

978-1-119-97660-8

BBIES

Growing Your Own Fruit & Veg
FOR DUMMIES

978-0-470-69960-7

Keeping Chickens
FOR DUMMIES

978-1-119-99417-6

Beekeeping
FOR DUMMIES

978-1-119-97250-1

Asperger's Syndrome For Dummies
978-0-470-66087-4

Basic Maths For Dummies
978-1-119-97452-9

Body Language For Dummies, 2nd Edition
978-1-119-95351-7

Boosting Self-Esteem For Dummies
978-0-470-74193-1

British Sign Language For Dummies
978-0-470-69477-0

Cricket For Dummies
978-0-470-03454-5

Diabetes For Dummies, 3rd Edition
978-0-470-97711-8

Electronics For Dummies
978-0-470-68178-7

English Grammar For Dummies
978-0-470-05752-0

Flirting For Dummies
978-0-470-74259-4

IBS For Dummies
978-0-470-51737-6

Improving Your Relationship For Dummies
978-0-470-68472-6

ITIL For Dummies
978-1-119-95013-4

Management For Dummies, 2nd Edition
978-0-470-97769-9

Neuro-linguistic Programming For Dummies, 2nd Edition
978-0-470-66543-5

Nutrition For Dummies, 2nd Edition
978-0-470-97276-2

Organic Gardening For Dummies
978-1-119-97706-3

FOR DUMMIES®

Making Everything Easier!™

UK editions

SELF-HELP

978-0-470-66541-1

978-1-119-99264-6

978-0-470-66086-7

STUDENTS

978-0-470-68820-5

978-0-470-974711-7

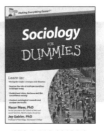

978-1-119-99134-2

HISTORY

978-0-470-68792-5

978-0-470-74783-4

978-0-470-97819-1

Origami Kit For Dummies
978-0-470-75857-1

Overcoming Depression For Dum
978-0-470-69430-5

Positive Psychology For Dummie
978-0-470-72136-0

PRINCE2 For Dummies, 2009 Edit
978-0-470-71025-8

Project Management For Dummi
978-0-470-71119-4

Psychometric Tests For Dummies
978-0-470-75366-8

Renting Out Your Property For
Dummies, 3rd Edition
978-1-119-97640-0

Rugby Union For Dummies, 3rd E
978-1-119-99092-5

Sage One For Dummies
978-1-119-95236-7

Self-Hypnosis For Dummies
978-0-470-66073-7

Storing and Preserving Garden
Produce For Dummies
978-1-119-95156-8

Study Skills For Dummies
978-0-470-74047-7

Teaching English as a Foreign
Language For Dummies
978-0-470-74576-2

Time Management For Dummies
978-0-470-77765-7

Training Your Brain For Dummies
978-0-470-97449-0

Work-Life Balance For Dummies
978-0-470-71380-8

Writing a Dissertation For Dumm
978-0-470-74270-9

FOR DUMMIES®

Making Everything Easier!™

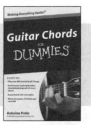

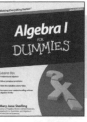

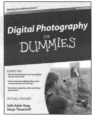

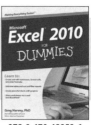